Introducing Aesthetics

Introducing Aesthetics

David E. W. Fenner

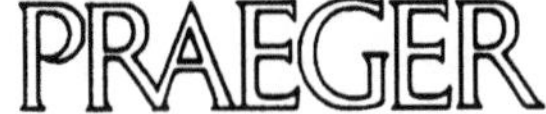

Westport, Connecticut
London

Library of Congress Cataloging-in-Publication Data

Fenner, David E. W.
    Introducing aesthetics / by David E. W. Fenner.
        p. cm.
    Includes bibliographical references and index.
    ISBN 0-275-97907-5 (alk. paper)—ISBN 0-275-97908-3 (pbk. : alk. paper)
    1. Aesthetics. 2. Art—Philosophy. I. Title.
    BH39.F459   2003
    111'.85—dc21   2002190863

British Library Cataloguing in Publication Data is available.

Library of Congress Catalog Card Number: 2002190863

ISBN: 0-275-97907-5
        0-275-97908-3 (pbk.)

First published in 2003

Praeger Publishers, 88 Post Road West, Westport, CT 06881
An imprint of Greenwood Publishing Group, Inc.
www.praeger.com

Printed in the United States of America

The paper used in this book complies with the
Permanent Paper Standard issued by the National
Information Standards Organization (Z39.48–1984).

10 9 8 7 6 5 4 3 2 1

For my parents,
George and Guadalupe Fenner

Contents

Introduction

This is a great time to be reading about aesthetics and the philosophy of art. This generation is in a unique historical position to appreciate the most challenging developments in art. We stand at what one of the world's leading aestheticians and art critics, Arthur Danto, calls the "end of art" (1986). This is in part because art apparently has challenged all that it can, and the result has been a virtual erasure of the line between real life and art, between practical objects and art objects. Whether or not Danto is right, much has happened in art in the past two centuries, and here at the end of the 20th century, and the beginning of the 21st, we have an unparalleled vantage point to study just what these developments have been and have meant. Aesthetics—the philosophy of beauty and art, the philosophy of the sensuous aspects of experience—has managed, through the diligence of aestheticians like Danto, to stay with the unfolding of the history of art, to try to answer the fascinating questions this history has offered.

In the Western tradition of philosophy, aesthetics began around the 4th century B.C. with Plato and Aristotle. But except for theories coming out of Neoplatonism and from a few medieval philosophers like St. Augustine and St. Thomas Aquinas, aesthetics did not command the interest of scholars or regain an audience until the Enlightenment, or, roughly, the time following the Renaissance. This should come as little surprise, since the philosophy of art has, and probably should, follow the life of art and the art world.

Our Western historical tradition, for which this text tries to provide a thorough but summary introduction—a *road map* of sorts—finds continuity between the work of the ancient Greeks and the work of the British Empiricists.

From this tradition we attempt to find answers to the traditional questions of aesthetics:

What does it mean to experience an object aesthetically?

What is art?

What is good art?

What is beauty?

How do we *know* what is aesthetically good or beautiful?

What do artworks mean?

What is and what should be the role of the art critic?

What are the roles of morality, patriotism, religion and truth in art?

What, if anything, should we censor? and on and on.

From the late 1600s to the late 1700s the British Empiricists—Shaftesbury, Hutcheson, Addison, Alison, Kames, Hume, Burke, Gerard—worked for the most part to find answers to the questions of *taste:* how it is that we can and do *know* that a thing, an object or an event, is beautiful or aesthetically good? During the later stages of this work, and just after it, the Western tradition moves from Britain to Germany. There (actually in Prussia), Immanuel Kant pursued the question of taste. He was followed by the Romantics Schopenhauer and Nietzsche. And from that point we move from the heart of Modern aesthetics to Contemporary aesthetics, with figures such as Tolstoy, Dewey, Santayana, Croce, and Collingwood bridging the 19th and 20th centuries.

But it is in the 20th century that the real fun begins, when art and artists raise challenge after challenge to what art was or what the institution of art, the "academy," had held art to be. Abstract Expressionism, Dadaism, Pop Art, and artistic movement after artistic movement—in New York, in Paris, in London—forced us to rethink how we viewed the nature of art. Is there, we asked ourselves, an *essence* to art? Is there some nature of art we can articulate, some formula or definition we can give, that expresses what art is? With the work of such artistic luminaries as Marcel Duchamp, Andy Warhol, Robert Rauschenberg, and Claes Oldenburg, we moved from seeing art as distinct from the ordinary to seeing art as *inclusive* of the ordinary—of ordinary objects like beds, soup cans, and snow shovels.

This prompted some aestheticians—such as Morris Weitz and Paul Ziff—to deny that there is any single nature of art. We can, they thought, come up with no suitable definition of art, because whatever art is now, it will not be tomorrow. If 'art' is the collection or compilation of all (bona fide) 'artworks', and the world is ready to include as art such objects as were being offered by Duchamp (show shovels, urinals, etc.), then 'art' is no longer easily described.

This challenge—the Antiessentialist challenge that no essence of art can be identified—spurred the philosophic community to action (rather, to *thought*). Aestheticians living today like Danto and George Dickie began to focus not on art as a collection of artworks but rather as traditions or institutions. Danto focused on the history of art, the tradition of art, and thereby came up with something all art had in common: all art has a place in what he calls the "Artworld." Dickie focused on the institution of art, the institution of people who see art, who display art, who create art, and found that this institution bound together the variety of objects and events we consider art.

So it is truly an exciting time to read aesthetics, because we are at such an incredible time in the history of art. Challenges have been raised, and answers have been offered. And now the student of aesthetics has an opportunity to view the panorama and decide for herself. The traditional questions of aesthetics do not go away. They are perennial. And *this* is what answers the question, *Why read or think about aesthetics?* Questions abound—inside and outside the ivory towers of the academy. But the answers offered today to those persistent questions are varied and many. And the options offered to the reader of aesthetics are rich indeed.

I have only one other task before we begin an examination of the Western tradition of aesthetics: to say a word about the "Western" tradition. Surely there has been much philosophically that has been said about art and beauty, and a great deal of it is outside or on the periphery of the Western tradition. One need only look to the vastness of the history of art of eastern Asia to recognize that there is much more to philosophizing about art than is captured just in the West. I mention this for two reasons. First, this book will not cover the breadth of all philosophizing about art. Indeed, serious doubts that such a task is even possible abound. Second, it is recommended to the serious aesthetic thinker than she consider looking into traditions outside of this one. It is limiting to think that the tradition one finds oneself in is all there is. The world is big, and the history of the world is bigger still. So *after* one reads this book, and *after* one understands this tradition—probably one's own—then one might think about looking at other resources, those that describe other traditions.

PART I

Experiences

CHAPTER 1

The Aesthetic Experience

"AESTHETIC"

We use the word "aesthetic" a great deal. We use the word most times as a modifier of "property," "object," "experience," "attitude," and "attention." The word "aesthetic" is used as both an adjective and as a noun, but when it is used as a noun, the word is offered as a shorthand description of an alternate, more precise description. For example, when an ordinary object is said to be "aesthetic," usually this means either (1) that the object is beautiful, elegant, balanced, and so forth—that is, it has some positive aesthetic quality—or (2) that the object offers one who would attend to it an aesthetic experience that is either readily available or rewarding in some way. The word is an adjective, and so to define the word is to define it as a modifier of some noun. The question now: Which noun?

The history of the word's usage goes back to Alexander Baumgarten, who began using the word in a philosophical context in 1735 to refer to a systemic attempt at a metaphysics or psychology of art. He believed that the foundations of the arts are "sensitive representations" that are not merely sensations but that are connected with feeling. Today we tend to think that aesthetics has to do with the sensuous aspects of experience. Of course, to say that aesthetics has to do with the sensuous aspects of experience is to give little in the way of an answer to students who want the word "aesthetic" defined. But at least it does narrow the field so that discussion may begin. To talk about the "sensuous aspects of experience" is to talk about experience. This seems an appropriate place to begin. Let me say why.

AESTHETIC EXPERIENCE AS BASIC

Consider "aesthetic" as a modifier of "attitude." Now, why start with "attitude"? A large philosophical tradition, spanning the 18th through the 20th centuries, focuses on the "aesthetic attitude." We will discuss the tradition in detail in the next chapter. This tradition focuses on the phenomenon of being able, through conscious and voluntary adoption of a particular viewpoint—the aesthetic attitude—to *turn on* the right conditions for being able to evaluate an object aesthetically or even to experience it aesthetically (different theorists aim for different goals).

Some time ago I purchased a recording entitled *Songs and Sounds of Orcinus Orca* (recorded by Paul Spong; produced by Ralph Harding; published by Total Recording of California, 1989). It is a collection of the sounds made by orcas, or killer whales, such as may be found at Sea World and off the northern Pacific coast. There are twelve cuts, each a recording of the whales during a particular activity or a particular mood. The recording was made by a scientist, but the descriptions that he attaches to the sounds range from scientific observation to music. The question is this: Are the sounds on this album music? Or are they simply interesting sounds appreciated as nature? Are they, if they are music, fantastic *songs* made by the some of largest creatures in nature? Are they a series of *communications*; are they like the sounds heard when one listens to an opera in a language not understood?

Whatever the initial answer, it seems clear that the answer is in large measure dependent upon *how one wishes* to listen to the sounds. If one is a zoologist, she might listen to these sounds in order to predict whale behavior as correlated with the sounds. If one is a linguist, he might be listening to find patterns. If one appreciates interesting music, she might be listening to the sounds purely for enjoyment as music. If one is a music critic, he might attend to the formal qualities of the sounds, to see if she can identify patterns, albeit perhaps patterns different from those sought by the linguists.

Besides the admission that one might, given different interests or purposes, be listening to the sounds in order to hear different things, as an ordinary person, *or as any of the specialists mentioned above*, one might easily hear the sounds in different ways. Such would probably be the case if someone suggested listening for patterns, the similarity to a faulty organ, the sublimity of the sounds of the largest creatures on earth, and so forth.

The importance of the question about *how* one is listening to these sounds lies in whether the experience of listening to these sounds is aesthetic in character or not. Furthermore, is it the case that whether the experience of these sounds is aesthetic or not—whether in some broad sense they are music or not—depends in great measure, perhaps completely so, on how the listener *chooses* to listen to the sounds? If the experience is aesthetic, it seems clear that it is not aesthetic because of something the *whales* are doing, except in the sense that it is to the *whales* that one is listening. It seems clear that if one is listening to the sounds and having an aesthetic experience, it is because the listener is attending to the sounds in a manner that renders the experience aesthetic. Since one is in the position to listen to the sounds in different ways, some of which seem patently unaesthetic and some (one?) of which seem to be aesthetic, the question about whether the sounds are constitutive of an aesthetic object seems to have something to do with what the listener is doing, something to do with what *attitude* the listener takes toward the sounds.

The philosophical tradition that focuses on understanding if there is an aesthetic attitude, and what it consists in, is nestled in England and Germany of the 18th and 19th centuries and America of the 20th. Originally the focus was on how one could go about making correct aesthetic judgments. Lord Shaftesbury, Francis Hutcheson, and Immanuel Kant believed that if one were to adopt the aesthetic attitude, one would be in the position to make correct aesthetic evaluations. This trend was replaced, through the work of such figures as Arthur Schopenhauer and, recently, Jerome Stolnitz, by a focus on the conditions for aesthetic experience. That is, instead of adopting the aesthetic attitude in order to make correct aesthetic judgments, the discussion turned to adoption of the aesthetic attitude in order to experience aesthetically—or, better, to have an aesthetic experience. The content of that experience would be some aesthetic object or event, made an aesthetic object or event merely by the act of viewing it from this aesthetic viewpoint, through adoption of the aesthetic attitude.

If this is an adequate quick overview of that tradition, it allows us to understand in a sort of hierarchy some of the nouns that "aesthetic" might modify. Aesthetic attention is attention directed toward aesthetic objects, events, or properties. Aesthetic objects and events are the content of aesthetic experiences. Aesthetic attitudes, or, better, *the* aesthetic attitude—if there is such a thing—is what allows us to have aesthetic experiences (which, even on the earlier view that adoption of an aesthetic attitude was for the purpose of aesthetic judgment, still places the having of an aesthetic experience logically earlier than attitude or judgment—that is, going on the supposition that one cannot make an aesthetic judgment in the absence of having an aesthetic experience). This leaves two things at the ground level in terms of discussing "the aesthetic": aesthetic properties and aesthetic experiences. I believe the latter is the more basic of the two.

If everyone has had aesthetic experiences—and this seems an uncontroversial assumption—then to some degree everyone can draw a line between those experience she has had that are aesthetic and those that are not. This line will probably be vague, but that does not matter. The point is not to draw the line so solidly that it can support a metaphysical discussion (of differences in kinds of experience) but to have the line be just strong enough to apportion some experiences from others. Then, in as strong or as loose terms as we wish and as our arguments will support, we can begin to say what is different about aesthetic experiences and nonaesthetic experiences.

THE AESTHETIC EXPERIENCE

Let me begin by saying that we must not suggest that every aesthetic experience will necessarily be positive or entail a favorable reaction. We might experience some object aesthetically and still have a negative experience. The habit of suggesting by claiming that something is *aesthetic* that it is *aesthetically good* is a matter of convenience, not a matter of definition. *Aesthetic* must cover the good *and* the bad, else we cut out an entire range of aesthetic experiences. Say that you dislike the work of Jackson Pollock. However, when you are in the gallery, looking at his work, you are appreciating it, or at least *experiencing* it, aesthetically. You are having an aesthetic experience. Now, because you find little value in his work, the experience you are having is not highly aesthetic, but it is, *since you are seeking an aesthetic experience*, aesthetic to some degree. So aesthetic experiences, like aesthetic objects, can be either good or bad or even indifferent.

There are several theories of what an—or *the*—aesthetic experience is. All of these theories have one thing in common: They attempt to describe what features all aesthetic experiences share. It is normally the case that when one attends a play, ballet, or opera, or visits a gallery, museum or garden, she calls her experiences aesthetic. When one fixes the car, brushes her teeth, or teaches a class, she does not normally label those experiences aesthetic. One can easily attend plays, operas, and the like and not have an aesthetic experience, so this is not to privilege these objects as aesthetic objects. Rather, I want to make the point that we commonly class some experiences off from others, labeling some aesthetic and others not. Whether or not one thinks that there is an *essence*, or a single nature, to aesthetic experiences, one may still separate the aesthetic experiences from the nonaesthetic ones.

For Clive Bell, the aesthetic experience occurs when one is experiencing in an object *Significant Form*. Bell's view is one of a tradition called *arousal theories*, where the point of the aesthetic experience is some state that the object is supposed to arouse in viewers. If an object has some important ingredient, then it will trigger a certain response in viewers, and that response, arousal proponents suggest, is *the* aesthetic experience. (We will discuss Bell's view in detail later in the book, since he primarily uses Significant Form as a means to define "art.")

For Jerome Stolnitz, the aesthetic experience is one characterized by *disinterest*. Stolnitz was a 20th-century aesthetic attitude theorist, and disinterest has been, over the course of aesthetic attitude theorizing, the most prevalent candidate for what the aesthetic attitude truly is. Stolnitz's goal was to expose the way in which aesthetic experience could be had, either at all or most fully. Stolnitz begins his account by noting that attention is selective. If our focus is practical, then we will focus on the functions of objects. If, however, our focus in not on purposeful, practical things, then that focus—that attitude—will be aesthetic. The focus in the absence of purpose is where one views the object as an aesthetic object, paying attention to its "phenomenal" properties—those properties that just have to do with how we sense the object—and to nothing further. One is not interested in what the object can do or accomplish. One is simply interested in the object on its own. This is what disinterest means, and this is, for Stolnitz, the nature of aesthetic experience.

John Dewey has perhaps, among early 20th-century philosophers, the deepest treatment of the aesthetic experience. For Dewey, the aesthetic experience is that experience that is maximally *unified*. All experiences, he suggests, are aesthetic to some degree, specifically the degree to which they are unified. Those individual experiences that are very unified constitute what Dewey calls *an* experience. And each experience that is *an* experience is an aesthetic experience. They are set apart, bounded, whole, complete—in a word, *unified*. Furthermore, unlike Stolnitz, Dewey conceives of an aesthetic experience that is very interactive between object and viewer. The viewer is very interested in the object of her aesthetic experience. This is at least on the surface different from Stolnitz's call to disinterest.

Finally, for this overview, there is Monroe Beardsley's account. Like Dewey, Beardsley makes the aesthetic experience focal in his treatment of aesthetics. Beardsley suggests that one is having an aesthetic experience if she is focused on the form and qualities of an object and this experience is unified and pleasurable. The particular qualities that we are looking for in the form of the object are *intensity, complexity* and *unity*, all tied together with pleasure. The aesthetic experience is had through paying attention to these items in the object, and having the experience of these aspects of the object be re-created in the mind of the viewer.

Beardsley suggests that experiences that are broadly aesthetic are parasitic in some sense on experiences of art. This is not to say that the appreciation of a flower or a sunset is had only after one has experienced some artwork(s). Through consideration of art we focus on what items make us most aesthetically pleased. These items are broadly classed under intensity, complexity, and unity. So it is these aspects that we seek out in natural aesthetic experience, or experiences of flowers and sunsets. The appreciation of art allows for a more precise definition or exploration of what we are looking for in natural aesthetic experiences.

Beardsley's list of aesthetic aspects does not grow out of some philosophical speculation, but out of a real accounting of what people look for in aesthetic situations. Beardsley's list is grounded empirically. His list of what constitutes an aesthetic experience is the following. For Beardsley, an experience that includes *some* of these is an aesthetic experience.

My present disposition is to work with a set of five criteria of the aesthetic character of experience...

    (1) Object Directness. A willingly accepted guidance over the succession of one's mental states by phenomenally objective properties (qualities and relations) of a perceptual or intentional field on which attention is fixed with a feeling that things are working or have worked themselves out fittingly.

> (2) Felt Freedom. A sense of release from the dominance of some antecedent concerns about past and future, a relaxation and sense of harmony with what is presented or semantically invoked by it or implicitly promised by it, so that what comes has the air of having been freely chosen.
>
> (3) Detached Affect. A sense that the objects on which interest is concentrated are set a little at a distance emotionally—a certain detachment of affect, so that even when we are confronted with dark and terrible things, and feel them sharply, they do not oppress but make us aware of our power to rise above them.
>
> (4) Active Discovery. A sense of actively exercising constructive powers of the mind, of being challenged by a variety of potentially conflicting stimuli to try to make them cohere; a keyed-up state amounting to exhilaration in seeing connections between percepts and between meaning, a sense (which may be illusionary) of intelligibility.
>
> (5) Wholeness. A sense of integration as a person, of being restored to wholeness from distracting and disruptive influences (but by inclusive synthesis as well as by exclusion), and a corresponding contentment, even through disturbing feeling, that involves self-acceptance and self-expansion. (1982, pp. 286, 288)

This is a detailed list, and it may not strike the casual reader as being obvious. But the very level of detail is in part the point of including it here. Beardsley's account of the aesthetic experience is probably the deepest one offered by aestheticians thus far.

Not everyone agrees with Beardsley, or the others, that there is such a thing as an aesthetic experience. George Dickie, Beardsley's most vocal critic on this matter, argues that there is *no* essential nature to the aesthetic experience. He claims that while aesthetic experiences might go on all the time, there is no such thing as *the* aesthetic experience. To suggest that there is a single character to the aesthetic experience is to invite counterexample, just as in the case of attempting to define art or beauty.

What the aesthetic experience proponent is attempting to do is to look at all of the experiences that we normally consider aesthetic—experiences of going to the opera, the ballet, a play, or a symphony; reading a novel or a poem; visiting a gallery, a museum, the seashore, or a garden—and then see if there is anything that is common to all of these. Is there a common nature to those experiences that we take to be aesthetic? Dickie argues that there is not.

Dickie argues that aesthetic experience is no different *in kind* from any other sort of experience. The experience of fixing a car or brushing one's teeth is essentially the same as the experience of watching a play or listening to a symphony. The difference is not in kind, but in *focus*. We attend to different properties or aspects of objects depending on our purpose in attending to them in the first place.

Even though he may be correct in denying that aesthetic experience is a separate kind of experience, there is still the question of how we distinguish and collect together aesthetic experiences. The experience of fixing cars or blenders may be classed according to the purpose had in attending, or it may be classed according to the properties to which one attends. But this sort of project—identifying aesthetic experiences on the basis of attending either to specific properties they have or with a certain purpose in mind—is contentious. Some, like Stolnitz, argue that attending to an object aesthetically is to attend to it without *any* regard for purpose.

Even though we might agree that it is unclear that there is an *essence* to aesthetic experience, we still find ourselves setting aesthetic experience off from other sorts of experience. So the search for commonality is valuable.

AESTHETIC PROPERTIES

I said above that aesthetic experiences are more basic than aesthetic properties. But I have not yet said much about what aesthetic properties are. Typically, an aesthetic property is a property of an object (or an event) that a person would cite (1) in defending or explaining his aesthetic evaluation of the object, or (2) in explaining what makes a particular experience aesthetic for him, or what engages him about a particular aesthetic object.

It is convenient to think of aesthetic properties in three levels. The top level is what Alan Goldman (1992) refers to as "pure value properties": "being beautiful, sublime, ugly, dreary." The middle level is made up of properties that seem aesthetically evaluative and are commonly cited as evidence for our top-level judgments. This middle level might include such terms as balanced, bold, clean, derivative, dull, elegant, garish, graceful, harmonious, moving, novel, original, powerful, realistic, trite, vivid, and whimsical. The bottom level is made up of "base" properties. These are the sorts of properties that anyone with working senses will pick up from the object. It is common to resort to citing these properties as evidence that the middle level properties one believes are present really are present. Base properties include color, line, texture, pattern, symmetry, and that sort of thing. Which base properties are relevant will depend on the artform, of course. One will naturally focus on different base properties when it comes to visual art, music, and literature.

Some might claim that base properties are really not aesthetic properties, and this brings up a very interesting dilemma. It is difficult, perhaps impossible, to circumscribe the set of aesthetic properties such that a single definition will capture what it is to be an aesthetic property. This seems true for several reasons. First, aesthetic properties seem to involve the use of taste or aesthetic evaluation. Frank Sibley (1959) made this point, and Beardsley made a similar one later (1973). When you pick out an aesthetic property, this seems to require you to appeal to your own aesthetic sensibilities, your taste. This means that an *objective* definition of aesthetic property will not be possible. It also means, if Sibley is right, that base properties are technically not aesthetic properties.

Second, if we allow in base properties as aesthetic properties, then it is unclear that we can ever say of any objective property that is involved in one's aesthetic experience that it is not an aesthetic property. So no property that *could* contribute to an person's aesthetic experience ought be dismissed as a (potential) aesthetic property. For instance, in knowing something of the conditions under which Mozart composed and of the instruments that were available to him, one's appreciation of his music could increase. Another example might be one's motivation to view a film more closely if it is known that the film had been nominated for an Oscar. This is not an unusual occurrence. To argue that some properties are not or cannot be aesthetic properties seems counterintuitive to what seems to be our goal in viewing aesthetic objects. One may not be interested in a boundary over which we must not tread in order to gain the best experience. We might well be interested in loosening boundaries so that whatever might contribute to the overall best experience might be admitted to our set of aesthetic properties.

Third, the 19th and 20th centuries are filled with art objects whose aesthetic character lies not much at all with the *sensuous* but with the *cognitive*. Marcel Duchamp's readymades—like his *In Advance of a Broken Arm*, which before it was an art object was an ordinary snow shovel, and his *Fountain*, which was originally a porcelain urinal—and John Cage's music—such as *4' 33"*, which is 4 minutes and 33 seconds of silence as a musician sits at a piano—are clear examples. Any definition of "aesthetic property," to encompass discussion of these sorts of artworks, cannot *merely* be a focus on the sensory. One cannot describe in *simply* objective terms the aesthetic properties of all those recent objects best labeled "conceptual art."

These sorts of considerations make defining "aesthetic property" in stable terms difficult, and perhaps impossible. This is why I said earlier that aesthetic experience is more basic than aesthetic properties. We cite aesthetic properties when we are trying to make sense of what makes an experience aesthetic. But the reverse does not seem true: just because a object has aesthetic properties does not automatically mean that we will experience it aesthetically. We will discuss this again when we get to chapter 3.

CHAPTER 2

The Aesthetic Attitude

SECTION ONE: DISINTEREST

Let's say that you and a friend have gone out to look at cars. You need to buy one. Now, what you are concerned with is having transportation to get you from home to work, and back again, perhaps taking weekend trips, and driving to your parent's house twice a year. So you study various aspects of the cars you are considering: Do they have good safety records? Good maintenance records? Good resale value? Good gas mileage? Are they affordable? Your friend, however, is not paying attention to these aspects of the cars you view. Instead, he pays attention to the color of the car, the lines of the car, the size, the shininess, the wood, the leather. He says that he believes that some of the cars you are considering are quite "aesthetic" while others are not.

Your central interest is not in how the car looks. You need a well-functioning and affordable car. However, when your friend points out the lines and color of the car, you shift your attention away from how functional the car is and to how "aesthetic" it is. Perhaps you notice that it is balanced and well proportioned and that the interior colors complement the exterior ones. But when your friend shows you how "aesthetic" the Jaguar is, your attention snaps back from how "aesthetic" the car is to how impractical it is—for you and others on a student budget.

This sort of shift, from being able to appreciate how "aesthetic" something is to being able to appreciate it simply as what is was made *for*, is the difference between taking the *aesthetic attitude* toward some object and taking an ordinary or practical attitude toward it. You can look at the cars in a variety of ways: as a mechanic, as a salesman, as a potential purchaser, as a highway patrol officer, *and* as an aesthetic viewer. Moreover, you can shift between these various perspectives. When you shift to the aesthetic view, then you take on, say proponents of this view, the *aesthetic attitude*. This shift has nothing to do with the *car*. The car, whether being viewed aesthetically or mechanically, stays the same. The change is in the viewer.

The trick is to determine what it means to take on the aesthetic attitude. It may seem obvious that the aesthetic viewer shifts mental states. It may also seem obvious that the aesthetic viewer shifts her focus of concentration. But what is this *new* mental state that the aesthetic viewer enters, and what is it upon which she *now* concentrates? Is there more than a single aesthetic attitude? Various theories have been advanced to determine the nature of the aesthetic attitude, beginning about the time of the Enlightenment and continuing to the present. In addition, various philosophers have challenged the notion of the aesthetic attitude, claiming that there is no such thing. We will review the most prominent positions of both camps.

The three most important views of what the aesthetic attitude is are: (1) the view that says that we need to be *disinterested* to experience aesthetically, as formulated by Immanuel Kant, Arthur Schopenhauer, and Jerome Stolnitz; (2) Edward Bullough's view that we need to establish a certain *Psychical Distance* between our consideration of the object and the object itself; and (3) Virgil Aldrich's view of "seeing as," or "seeing impressionistically." And the most important critic of the aesthetic attitude is George Dickie.

The aesthetic attitude is an attitude or state-of-perceiving entered into voluntarily and consciously by a viewer (or listener) that serves to (1) make the spectator receptive to the having of an aesthetic experience and (2) transform the object of the spectator's perception from an object-in-the-world into an aesthetic object. It is with this quite broad working definition in mind that we can proceed with our reviews. The first is of the tradition of disinterest.

DISINTEREST

Disinterest (or disinterestedness) has been, over the course of aesthetic attitude theorizing, the most prevalent candidate for what the aesthetic attitude is. It was first discussed by Lord Shaftesbury and Francis Hutcheson as they formulated their theories of beauty and taste. Both Shaftesbury and Hutcheson are thought to stand at the beginning of the tradition that emphasizes disinterest. (We will examine their views in detail in chapter 8, which deals with defining "beauty.") Disinterest was explored in depth by the German thinkers Immanuel Kant and Arthur Schopenhauer, and within the last 25 years, disinterest has been most prominently supported by Jerome Stolnitz. After discussing Kant and Schopenhauer, we will turn to the work of Stolnitz.

Our grouping of Stolnitz with the Germans of the 18th and 19th centuries is not to suggest that his view simply rehashes what they had already done. Indeed, Stolnitz's theory is much more streamlined than those of the Germans. In Stolnitz's account, there are no large metaphysical commitments as are present in the theories of the Kant and Schopenhauer. In spite of the many similarities, Stolnitz's view aimed at an end different from those of the Germans. The goal of Kant's program was convergent (or universal agreement among) aesthetic judgment and its explanation. The goal of Schopenhauer's program was to secure escape from the phenomenal and Willful world, to gain access to the Ideas and Will-lessness of the world behind the phenomenal. But the goal of Stolnitz's program is more modest and straightforward. He sought to examine the means of bringing about aesthetic experience. Stolnitz's goal is more in line with the goal of most, perhaps all, aesthetic attitude theorists today.

IMMANUEL KANT

Immanuel Kant's conception of disinterest focuses on disinterest *as an attitude necessary for the correct appraisal of whether something is beautiful.* Kant says that, among the many items that we must attend to in viewing aesthetically, we principally must be disinterested in the object in order to experience that object aesthetically. Now, this disinterest does not mean we ought to shun or ignore the object. Quite the opposite. The disinterest we apply to the experience is an *interested disinterest.* The problem in the paradoxical nature of the expression lies with defining disinterest.

'Disinterest', Kant tell us, refers to the actual existence of the object. We are viewing disinterestedly when we are viewing without any interest in the actual physical existence of the object. We ought view as if we did not care a bit about the object's physical existence; we ought care only about the appearance of the object (using 'appearance' broadly—it must also cover listening and other senses).

A second part of the definition of disinterest is found in the notion that we must be disinterested toward any function that the object might serve. In order to view disinterestedly, one must not look at the object as a tool or as anything else that could be useful. So while one might see Duchamp's *In Advance of a Broken Arm* (the show shovel) as a useful item were that object hanging in a garage in Maine in January, to see it aesthetically, to view it disinterestedly, one must take no notice of its use. One must concentrate only on it as an aesthetic object, that is, paying attention only to those elements of the experience of viewing the object that will provide a richer and more rewarding *aesthetic* experience.

Third, in viewing disinterestedly, we must not bring the object "under any category." We must treat the object on its own. So if Sam were to see a Manet, he ought not judge that work as a member of the class of Impressionist art, but rather he should treat the object as if it had no connection to any other object, real or imagined. In a sense, Sam must not look at the *external relations* that an aesthetic object might bear to other items in the world. He must only pay attention to the *internal relations*, those that exist as a matter of the *form* of the object and a matter of the features of the object itself.

Kant makes a rather important distinction between *liking disinterestedly* and merely *liking*. When we merely "like" an object, we like it as some means to something else. We like it because it can provide some pleasure for us—a *liking of the merely agreeable*—or we like it because it can serve some other purpose for us. We like it as an instrumental good, a good *for something else*. A disinterested liking, however, is a pure liking for its own sake. We do not like the object as an instrumental good, but we like it on its own.

These three features contribute to a true disinterested appreciation of an aesthetic object. We say "disinterested *appreciation*" because we must be keenly aware and focused on the image of the object, says Kant. One may, perhaps, be supremely disinterested in an object were she on the other side of the earth. However, this is, as we have seen, *not* what Kant had in mind. He did not mean *non*interested. His disinterest is a particular kind, and it contributes to aesthetic viewing only when the viewer is very interested—that is, very interested in the *image* of the object, on its own and by itself. In a sense then, Kant's notion of disinterest is only to block certain kinds of viewing. It is not a matter of how we should view. It is not a matter of giving us a formula that will provide us with aesthetic viewing. Instead, it is more a matter of telling us how we *ought not* view. And, if we do not view in the nonaesthetic ways, we put ourselves in the correct position, in the correct *attitude*, for viewing aesthetically. (We will discuss Kant's views in more detail in chapter 11, in defining "beauty.")

ARTHUR SCHOPENHAUER

It is from an understanding of Arthur Schopenhauer's metaphysics that we are best able to understand how his notion of disinterest allows us to view aesthetically. Two things are noteworthy here. First, Schopenhauer was a Platonist. He believed in the essences of things existing outside of the particular objects. Second, he believed in a Will, an all-encompassing world force that exists through want and desire. Schopenhauer articulates three ways to escape the Will. One can become an ascetic. One can become a philosopher. Or one can seek out aesthetic experiences. Through experiencing aesthetically, we access the Forms or Platonic essences. We rise above the physical world and can contemplate the spiritual world.

Considering art, viewing aesthetically, allows us to escape from the Will. And this escape from the Will is accomplished by viewing disinterestedly. In both cases, we are discussing the negative: we *escape* from the Will by viewing *dis*interestedly. So, in a serious sense, to view aesthetically is to view by *not* paying attention to certain things, by *ignoring* those elements of the world that contribute to want and desire. By ignoring the relations that an object has to other aspects of the world—the "where, when, why, and wither of things," said Schopenhauer—one can appreciate just the object itself, on its own, and contemplate what is most real in the object. He can concentrate on finding the Form (capital "F") in the object.

Now, unlike other aestheticians, Schopenhauer believed that our viewing disinterestedly, when we take on the aesthetic attitude of disinterest, actually *changes* the object we are viewing. We *transform* the object into something new: an aesthetic object. This is what makes Schopenhauer's theory of disinterest more truly an aesthetic attitude theory than others, such as Kant's. While there is some question about whether Kant fits squarely into the aesthetic attitude tradition (since he was primarily interested in aesthetic judgment, not simply aesthetic experiencing), there is no question that Schopenhauer fits, because for Schopenhauer the aesthetic attitude *changes* the object being viewed from a common object in the world into an aesthetic object.

Schopenhauer is one of the few attitude theorists who actually treats the aesthetic attitude in such a literal way with regard to changing the object into an aesthetic object. Most other attitude theorists simply mean that we pay attention to certain aspects, certain relations, certain properties that were always in the object, but when viewed nonaesthetically they are missed or hidden. Schopenhauer has the aesthetic viewer change the constitution, or the *objective status* of the object. This is partly accomplished because of the close relationship between the viewer and object that is had when the viewer attends disinterestedly. And while the viewer changes the object, the object in turn changes the viewer. It lifts him out of the ordinary world. It makes him, for a time, a resident of the spiritual or essential world.

So disinterest, or *ignoring* certain aspects of the object, accomplishes a great deal. (1) It allows the viewer to attend aesthetically. (2) It transforms the object from an ordinary object to an aesthetic object. (3) It allows the subject, under his own power, to rise above the world of individual objects and contemplate the real world of essences; a world that is free of Will.

We may take yet another step in leaving Will. Schopenhauer suggests that while proper contemplation of any aesthetic object will accomplish an escape from Will, it is through contemplation of a special art form that we most truly can escape Will. If we attend to *formalized music* we not only are in the position to contemplate the Forms, but we are also in the best position to escape the Will.

Certainly there may be problems with Schopenhauer's account (as there seem to be, of course, with almost all philosophical accounts). However, there are not so many as one might initially believe. His metaphysics is complex and would commit us to the existence of two worlds, a natural one and a supernatural one. Also, there is the concept of the Will and the commitment to belief in such a force, especially for scientific-minded students of the late 20th century. However, the core of a strong and successful aesthetic attitude theory is left much intact *even if we do not adopt his metaphysics*. The key issues of (1) being able to experience aesthetically and (2) changing the object from an ordinary object into an aesthetic object are still present even with a rejection of the heavy metaphysics. And these elements are, over the course of the attitude traditions, the most central to the attitude theorizing. Moreover, Schopenhauer has a definite approach, that of disinterest. He fits well into the attitude tradition. (We will discuss Schopenhauer's views in more detail in chapter 4, in defining "art.")

JEROME STOLNITZ

Jerome Stolnitz has been the chief 20th-century defender of the traditional conception of disinterest. Two things, however, distinguish him from Kant and Schopenhauer: (1) He does not have a metaphysics in which the disinterest is supposed to fit; and (2) he does not specifically address aesthetic evaluation or judgment in his description of disinterest (as did Kant). Stolnitz is interested in what conditions are necessary for the aesthetic experience, so his interest is broadly psychological or mental.

Stolnitz begins his account by noting that attention is selective. We focus, either consciously or routinely, on different aspects of what meets our senses, and we dismiss aspects that are not relevant to our purpose of viewing. If our purpose is to purchase a car, we focus on the function of the cars we view. In the absence of purpose, however, we focus on the car not as a car per se. When we view without purpose we focus on the object as an aesthetic object, paying attention to its phenomenal properties and to nothing further.

Stolnitz defines the aesthetic attitude as (1) disinterested and (2) sympathetic attention to any object. Like Kant, Stolnitz suggests that we ought not, in viewing an object aesthetically, attend to any *purpose* that the object might serve, but pay attention only to the object for and it itself. We must view the object not as an instrumental good, but as an end in itself.

But what about the notion of *sympathy*? Stolnitz contends that if we are to appreciate the object, we must accept it on its own terms. That is, in order to experience the object unpurposefully and aesthetically, we must pay attention only to the features of the object, and we must pay attention closely and carefully. We must be sympathetic to the work, else *disinterest* might well mean *lack of interest*, which is exactly what we do not want. As it did with Kant, it may sound like a paradox that we must be interested in the work in order to maintain a disinterest in the work, but the fact is that if we do not have some initial interest then we are not at all in the position to appreciate the work—or, more precisely, to experience the work aesthetically. The paradox dissolves when we understand "interest" as "sympathy" and "disinterest" as "the absence of purpose."

Stolnitz also carries into the 20th century Schopenhauer's idea that the spectator's attitude transforms the object from an object-in-the-world into an aesthetic object. Here, we do not mean that the object undergoes an *objective* change, as it may according to Schopenhauer. We mean that the object's properties that would lead to a full aesthetic experience—its qualities of lines, shapes, colors, symmetry, balance, harmony, and so forth—are *hidden* until the aesthetic attitude is adopted by the viewer toward the object.

Viewing the object without regard to purpose is *not* to say that any knowledge about the object, such as who created it, when, and under what conditions, is irrelevant. If knowledge about an object *helps* in our aesthetic experiencing of the object—facilitates our appreciation, or makes our appreciation more rich and rewarding—then this knowledge is allowed. On the other hand, Stolnitz allows for the viewer and her experience of the work to dictate, at least for her, the depth or range of the aesthetic qualities of the object. If the critic disagrees, nothing follows; the viewer has no reason to change his view in the face of disagreement. This is not a surprising twist. Although Stolnitz is not interested in dismissing the critics, he is interested, as most aesthetic attitude theorists are, in putting the focus on the actual experience of the viewer.

One might object to Stolnitz's statement that paying attention to an object's properties for the purpose of having an aesthetic experience *is* paying attention with a particular purpose in mind. In aesthetic viewing, the motive or initial purpose is to notice the aesthetic features of the object, or, more precisely, to have an aesthetic experience. Since the aesthetic attitude of disinterested and sympathetic attention can be easily differentiated conceptually from aesthetic experiencing, it is hard to see how the aesthetic attitude could avoid being purposeful in the sense that its purpose is to foster aesthetic experiencing. This paradox does not dissolve as easily as the paradox of "interested disinterest." We enter the aesthetic attitude *in order to have* an aesthetic experience. But perhaps Stolnitz means "no *ulterior* purpose" should be had.

DISINTEREST CONSIDERED

There are several criticisms of disinterest in the literature on the aesthetic attitude. One made popular by George Dickie is the view that it seems that one can be both viewing aesthetically—that is, paying attention to the aesthetic features of the object—while still paying attention to some external relation of the object, some aspect of the object that has something to do with some other part of the world. For instance, we can pay attention to both the aesthetic feature of a work *and* to the moral point of view of the object (if it has one). Stolnitz might say that if we are disturbed by the moral point of view of Anthony Burgess's *A Clockwork Orange*, we will not be able to appreciate the work aesthetically. But sometimes, as in *Clockwork*, the moral point of view is essential to a full understanding or appreciation of the work.

What saves Stolnitz here is the phrase "if we are disturbed." You will recall that above we mentioned that *knowledge about an object* is acceptable if it contributes to either the having of or richness of the aesthetic experience. In *Clockwork* the moral point of view seems essential to a full appreciation of the work. Perhaps the idea that we can include the moral point of view is that we must view sympathetically. But the point is still present: it would seem that we do not merely need disinterest to have the best aesthetic experience, but sometimes that aesthetic experience comes by having *other* attitudes as well, such as moral, religious or political attitudes.

This feeds into another criticism of the attitude of disinterest. Sometimes being *interested* can *contribute* to the aesthetic experience. Take the following example: Sally is in a horror film. This particular film is based on the Biblical accounts of the Apocalypse and the end of the world. (Perhaps the film is the *Omen.*) Sally might be able to appreciate the film well while still being main- taining disinterest toward it, as prescribed by Kant, Schopenhauer, or Stol- nitz. She might even be able to appreciate the film more if she takes moral or even religious attitudes toward it as well. But what if Sally takes a personal interest in the film? What if Sally takes the very personal—and it would seem very interested—attitude that what she is viewing is *really* what will happen in the final days? Suppose that Sally is a Christian and naive, perhaps, to the embellishments on the Scriptures that the director or writer engages in. She may well feel that she is viewing a pre-record, a prophetic account, of what will actually take place at the end of time. She would, it stands to reason, be rather more terrified than she would be were she simply following the disin- terest prescription. If the success of a horror film is in part based on how frightened it makes its viewers, and the greatest aesthetic experience regard- ing a horror film is to feel maximally frightened, then to be disinterested toward the film—disinterested *at all*—might be to harm the power of the film and settle for a less robust aesthetic experience.

In any event, disinterest as a formulation of the aesthetic attitude is and has been the most popular formulation throughout the history of attitude theo- rizing. Even today, more aestheticians sympathetic to the notion of the aes- thetic attitude would align themselves with the disinterest camp.

SECTION TWO: RECENT VIEWS

Two 20th-century aesthetic attitude theories are those of Edward Bullough and Virgil Aldrich. We will explore them here.

EDWARD BULLOUGH'S PSYCHICAL DISTANCE

The notion of Psychical Distance originated in a 1912 article by Edward Bullough, published in the *British Journal of Psychology*. It was called "'Psychical Distance' as a Factor in Art and as an Aesthetic Principle." It is interesting that the article was put out as a piece of psychology rather than philosophy. This may be relevant to our discussion later.

Bullough's work is considered by Stolnitz to be another exploration of disinterest as a candidate for the aesthetic attitude. In addition to sharing many points of support, the two accounts also are susceptible to similar criticisms. But it is important to see their differences too. Bullough's article has enjoyed enormous influence. It has been written about and read about in scholarly journals and discussion, of course. But beyond this, Bullough's term 'Psychical Distance' or its diminutive 'Distance' has made it into everyday language. Though relatively young, Psychical Distance has enjoyed more pervasive effect than has the more time-honored notion of disinterest—that is, since the time Bullough wrote the article.

It is not uncommon to hear someone in a gallery or at a film or play speak of needing to maintain some Distance from the object in order to appreciate it correctly. No doubt part of the reason for this is the nature of 20th-century art itself; it invites controversy over its meaning or message or whether it is even art in the first place. And 'Distance' is commonly invoked as a prescription for an unenthusiastic viewer to become a bit more receptive to the object, as art or as an aesthetic object, he is attempting to experience aesthetically. Granted, the advice might be to invoke *physical* distance—as one might advise with an impressionistic painting—but on many occasions, the advice to acquire distance is similar to advice to acquire *objectivity*.

Bullough suggests that in order to experience an object aesthetically, the subject must Distance herself from the object. She must attend without regard for the practical. But more than this, *'Distance' is that state such that you understand that you—your person, your emotions, the potential of your action—are not actually engaged directly with the object.* You are out of direct involvement with the object, experiencing it as if it were out of your reach. And the object cannot effect any changes in you; your experience of the object may result in changes in you—such as heightened awareness, sadness, joy, or rage—but these changes are possible only as states that you retain control over, which your attendance allows. (It is on these grounds that we can see the most plain difference between *Distance* and *disinterest*. *Distance* has to do with the *effects* of art object to viewer, and vice versa; *disinterest* has to do with which *aspects* of the art object should properly be the objects of attention and consideration.)

It may seem to follow, then, that the object itself has to cooperate for Distance to properly take place. Objects that are inherently directly engaging of the observer seem not to be objects that are conducive to being experienced aesthetically because they are not objects that are conducive to your experiencing them with Distance. This is, on the face of things, a major contrast between Psychical Distance and disinterest or any traditional formulation of the aesthetic attitude. However, while it is certainly easier to maintain this mutual responsibility for the occurrence of Distance, *Distance* might easily be reworked, especially in light of what may be its parent theory, disinterest, such that one might potentially take an attitude of Distance toward anything, even if that thing were not cooperative in one's effecting Distance between himself and the object.

For instance, it is hard to see how Sam might remain Distanced if an art object punched him in the nose; however, it is not beyond imagination to conceive his taking a punch in the nose and thinking to himself, "I see that this punch in the nose is an integral part of the unfolding of this play, and so I will not retaliate, but will attempt to understand the punch in the nose, or feel about the punch in the nose, in a way that is commensurate with appreciation of the unfolding of the play." Now for him to do so might be a bit odd (a bit?), but such a thing can be imagined. And the upshot of this example is to point out the ambiguity of whether the object to be experienced aesthetically must cooperate in some way with effecting Distance. The ambiguity is less severe in light of the ancestry of disinterest and what was defined early on as the traditional formulation of the aesthetic attitude, that is, that it may be applied to any object whatsoever.

This detached affect definition of Psychical Distance seems, given the psychological source of the notion, a fairly accurate one. If Distance is an attitude that is psychologically—that is, empirically—found to be the state that people are in when they are most obviously attentive to the aesthetic features of a work, then the definition must be capable of empirical confirmation.

Bullough's conception of aesthetic experiencing admits of degree. One can be more Distanced or less. (This is another clear difference between *Distance* and *disinterest*. *Disinterest* does not admit of degree.) This is important because Bullough explains to us that to be Distanced is in itself *not* sufficient for aesthetic experiencing, at least aesthetic experiencing of the most robust sort. Bullough introduces what he calls his *Antinomy of Distancing: In order for the fullest or best aesthetic experience to take place, one must seek not only to Distance herself from the work, but she must also seek to keep that Distance to an absolute minimum*. While Distance is necessary, the least possible amount is optimal for the best aesthetic experiencing. Bullough calls this an antinomy and aptly so. It would seem that the *least* amount of distance would closely approach having none at all; but Bullough requires that we maintain at least some.

Most of Bullough's examples come from the theatre, and his example to demonstrate the Antinomy is no exception. Bullough asks us to imagine that we are at a production of *Othello*. Now, in order to properly appreciate it, it must be the case that we understand that we are not to run on stage to stop Othello from strangling Desdemona. This is an instantiation of Distance between ourselves and the play. However, simply to be Distanced is not sufficient. We also must be (1) attentive to the play and (2) be in sympathy with the play, attempting to understand it, and feel the emotions that are appropriate— that the play traditionally has brought out in attentive and interested audiences. In short, we must not only be Distanced, but we also must be *sympathetic* to the play. We must attain the Distance, and we ought to attain the least amount of Distance without losing it. So it is appropriate to feel despair when watching Macbeth receive the news of his wife's death; it is appropriate to feel sorrow when Lear finds that Cordelia has been killed; it is appropriate to feel frustration when Juliet hears that she is to marry Paris.

Our appropriate reaction to what is happening on stage—or in a painting, or in a symphony, or in a novel—is necessary to our full aesthetic appreciation of the object. But it is important to note that if we are consistent in our belief that the aesthetic attitude can be taken to any object at any time, then we must note that the reaction we experience is not an instance of our being controlled by the object. For instance, one may see dew-covered flowers on the way to the office every morning and think nothing more than that her shoes are probably getting damp. But she might stop, attend to a group of the flowers in a Distanced manner, and notice that in doing so, she can appreciate them aesthetically *and* notice that they look sad, weighed down from the dew. She might feel melancholy in response. So a case is easily made for fitting Bullough's Distance into the traditional view of the aesthetic attitude.

Before leaving the subject of his Antinomy, it is important to note the close similarity between Bullough's account of optimal aesthetic experiencing and Stolnitz's theory about the aesthetic attitude. Bullough seems essentially to say that necessary and sufficient conditions for our experiencing aesthetically are (1) that we are Distanced, (2) that we attend to the object, and (3) that we do so with the least amount of Distance. Stolnitz's conditions essentially are (1) that we are disinterested, (2) that we attend to the object, and (3) that we do so sympathetically, taking the object on its own terms. The parallel here is striking. Not only are the Distancing and the disinterest so similar, but the instruction to view with the least amount of Distance and the instruction to view sympathetically are similar as well. Stolnitz mentions that it is important to note that aesthetic viewing is not instantiated in a cowlike stare, and Bullough gives us fundamentally the same opinion. It is necessary, as we explored in our treatment of Stolnitz, that this be included. Inattention to, or apathy toward, an object can render our experience of that object either completely nonaesthetic or of a very low aesthetic quality. The cowlike star for Stolnitz is what Bullough calls over-Distancing.

An interesting criticism of Distance comes from Suzanne Langer, whose account is in her book *Feeling and Form*. Langer recalls that as a child she saw a production of *Peter Pan*. In the plot, there comes a point where the fairy Tinkerbell drinks some poison in order to prevent Peter from drinking it himself. Tinkerbell becomes very ill and is close to death. Peter, in desperation, appeals to *the audience* to assist him in saving Tinkerbell's life; if they would clap vigorously it would help Tinkerbell recover. At this intrusion, Langer reports, she was horrified and miserable, because the magic and illusion of the production was ruptured when the Distance with which she was attending the production was lost. This supposedly shows that Distance is necessary to proper aesthetic viewing. However, the support for her point is lost when Langer admits that among all children around her, *she was the only one who did not respond enthusiastically and joyfully.*

There are many examples of artworks—bona fide artworks—that call for the inclusion of the spectator as participant in the aesthetic object. Counterexamples, like the *Peter Pan* case, can be found aplenty. One example is Andrew Lloyd Webber's *Cats*. In the theatre, when the cats are not dancing or singing on stage, they roam around the audience, soliciting the audience to pet them and show them where the litter box is. When one is petting an actor, it is hard to imagine oneself Distanced from the production.

A second sort of counterexample to Psychical Distance is when the object, instead of involving the audience through negating Distance, creates over-Distancing between itself and the spectator. An intriguing example of this is Tom Stoppard's *The Real Thing*, where the production begins with a play inside of the main play. In characteristic Stoppard style, the audience does not know that the play they initially see on stage is a play inside the play. When they realize this, they are taken aback. One finds herself at a great Distance from the original play (the play inside the play).

Another example of this is the play *M. Butterfly*. The principle character, Pinkerton, continually breaks from the action of the play to explain to the audience what is going on, in both the sequence of events and his own mind. During this time, he might change costumes, and the famous Chinese Property Men might change the set. The audience finds itself over-Distanced from the actual play, in listening to Pinkerton and watching the set changers.

Perhaps a simpler example of purposeful over-Distancing comes from television. In the long-running ABC sitcom *Growing Pains*, the son asks the father, "How often do I bring my problems to you, anyway?" and the father replies, "Every Wednesday evening, eight, seven Central." These breaks from Distance are included to add to the cleverness of the object, and if successful, the cleverness or breaking Distance can heighten the aesthetic enjoyment of the object.

The parallels between Distance and disinterest are many. Each account includes similar conditions: attention, sympathy, and (simply put) disconcern for practical matters. Each has similar points of support, and the 20th-century formulations (Bullough's and Stolnitz's) each take the aesthetic experience as the goal of adopting Distance or disinterest. Each, it was argued, fit into the traditional formulations of what an aesthetic attitude is; that is, principally, Distance or disinterest may be applied by an agent to *any* object.

It seems plausible to view Distance as a psychological stepchild of disinterest. Given this interpretation, Bullough's program is susceptible to all the criticisms of the notion of disinterest. But this is not a symmetrical relationship; the criticisms advanced against Distance are not so clearly criticisms of disinterest, and the central reason for this is the narrowness of Bullough's program.

VIRGIL ALDRICH'S IMPRESSIONISTIC VISION

Virgil Aldrich is perhaps, after the traditional theorists, the most influential of the aesthetic attitude theorists of the 20th century. His view, though, because it is motivated so differently, is markedly different from those that we have discussed previously. What disturbs Aldrich about the traditional attitude theories is that they place such a great emphasis on the viewer for producing the aesthetic character of the object. It is the viewer, traditionally, by means of her *turning on* her aesthetic attitude to the object, who transforms that object from an ordinary object to an aesthetic object. Aldrich's motivation was to bring to the notion of aesthetic viewing more objectivity than had been captured in other accounts.

Aldrich posits two separate ways of viewing. The first way is called *observation*. By 'observation' Aldrich means the sort of viewing that focuses on the practical. The second sort is what Aldrich calls "viewing aspectually" or "prehending" (or "prehension"). For Aldrich, observation is viewing the intrinsic characteristics of an object, and viewing them only as a scientist or (say) a machine would. This is *not* the way the aesthetic viewer views the object, however. The aesthetic viewer "prehends" the object, doing so by seeing the *objective* qualities of the figure, but seeing them aspectually or impressionistically. She sees them as they are representative of something that is different but that has objectively the same qualities.

Aldrich's motivation is to ensure as complete an objectivity as he can, while still maintaining that there is a difference in kind between viewing ordinarily and viewing aesthetically. To fulfill the first condition, that of objectivity, he says that the exact same objective properties that the scientist would see are the properties that the aesthetic viewer sees. And to fulfill the second condition, distinguishing between observation and prehension, he says that through our viewing the one set of properties differently we prehend in the objective properties different objects. When we look at a cloud, we might apply the mundane label 'cloud', but we might also apply more creative labels, such as 'dragon' or 'train' to what we *objectively* see.

But we may now have a problem. What does this have to do with aesthetic viewing as typified by looking at paintings, listening to symphonies, or reading novels? If the connection between Aldrich's prehension account and the way we normally experience typical aesthetic vehicles, such as artworks, is not or cannot be made, the account suffers.

There is another reason why Aldrich's account may suffer. The notion of objectivity seems watered down, perhaps too much so. Part of the reason for his *objective* account was to ensure that some impressions of an artwork could be judged incorrect. But does he succeed in providing a *criterion of correctness*? If Sally sees a cloud that Sam asserts is a house with smoke coming from the chimney and that Susan asserts is a locomotive with smoke coming from the stack, who is to say that Sid is not prehending correctly when he asserts sincerely that it looks like a frog on a lily pad or a bologna sandwich? Sid is free, *so long as he can really see what he asserts to see*, to have the objective properties of the material object form such a large number of aesthetic objects, of impressions, that one can virtually claim an infinite set of these. *Objective* or "what's really there, *apart* from the subject" may constitute a very large set, and so the objectivity that Aldrich was attempting to capture is inert. So long as the viewer is sincere, he can claim almost anything to be objectively there.

THE AESTHETIC ATTITUDE CONSIDERED

Is there such a thing as the aesthetic attitude? There certainly seems to be, because it is difficult to explain otherwise how we can view objects at one time as nonaesthetic and at another as aesthetic. Perhaps, though, the aesthetic attitude is not meant to describe how we see *everything* aesthetically that we take to be aesthetic, but is only supposed to describe this special "on-off" phenomenon. That is, perhaps the aesthetic attitude is not *necessary* for aesthetic viewing, but, if entered into, it is *sufficient* for viewing aesthetically (if you take on the aesthetic attitude, you're guaranteed to experience aesthetically, but you don't have to adopt the aesthetic attitude to have an aesthetic experience).

It is a fairly common phenomena that aesthetic attitude theories seemingly cannot explain. Have you ever been hurrying to class, perhaps a bit late, and out of the blue you are struck with the beauty of the courtyard or university green or classroom building? It is not uncommon for beauty to *break in upon us*, and while this certainly happens less in situations where we are rushing or where we are preoccupied, it still occurs. This immediate impact of beauty on us is not explained through an attitude theory. In an attitude theory, one must consciously and volitionally take on—or turn on—the aesthetic attitude. No such time or volition is present in the cases of beauty breaking in on us. This is why while taking on the aesthetic attitude may be sufficient for aesthetic viewing—that it is enough that we view aesthetically every time we take on that attitude—it may not be necessary, given that we may experience aesthetically even without taking on this special attitude.

In any event, it is clear that none of the formulations of the aesthetic attitude we have here described are completely without problem. While they all have their respective merits, they also all have problems. Again, this is not to suggest that we dump all talk of the attitude. The problems are merely challenges for further thought, consideration, and work. Philosophy proceeds through careful thought. With nearly every philosophic topic, more thought is necessary. It presents a challenge and an opportunity for the student of philosophy—in our case aesthetics—to continue the work by contributing his or her own thoughts on the subject.

PART II

Objects and Events

CHAPTER 3

The Aesthetic Object

An *aesthetic object* is any object or event that is the focus of aesthetic attention or the focus of an aesthetic experience. We might say further that aesthetic objects are typically objects like paintings, symphonies, plays, flowers, sunsets, and so forth. In principle, however, an aesthetic object can be *any* sensible ("able to be sensed") object in the world. This is because any sensible object in the world can be attended to or experienced aesthetically.

In trying to narrow what we allow to be an aesthetic object, we might attempt something like the following: aesthetic objects are only those objects that we either normally experience aesthetically or that provide for us good aesthetic experiences. The first part of this, "normally experience aesthetically," is too vague to be of use. (1) What Sam *normally experiences aesthetically* may be different from what Sally *normally experiences aesthetically*, and (2) even if we can pin down what is "normal" and what is not, why should that function as a definition of an aesthetic object *if* one has the best aesthetic experiences through attention to something that does not, on this definition, qualify as an aesthetic object? And from the second part of this, "provide for us *good* aesthetic experiences," it follows that there can be no *bad* aesthetic objects. If an object must provide a positive experience, this disallows objects we believe to be aesthetic that might provide us with bad or perhaps lukewarm aesthetic experiences. Perhaps we all agree that sunsets and flowers are classic examples of aesthetic objects, and perhaps we say that these objects generally provide for us good aesthetic experiences. But what about the disarray on the desk? Can we not view that aesthetically? Can the messy desk be an aesthetic object, given that we appreciate what it is *lacking*, that is, order? This is certainly not meant to suggest that the above definitions be taken seriously. These simple definitions are raised in order to show difficulties with attempting to limit what may count as an aesthetic object.

Any narrowing of our definition of what is an aesthetic object will meet with problems. However, we ought not embrace a definition that is too broad. For instance, though we may agree that an aesthetic object *can* be any object in the world, it would be odd to maintain that all objects in the world *are* aesthetic objects. While the *potential* of their being experienced aesthetically is quite real—that is, we may be able to experience any object in the world aesthetically—without some sort of *actualization* of that potential, it seems inappropriate to call these things aesthetic objects.

One may see desks, chairs, clocks, computers, and books all day long. It is rare that one experiences any of these objects aesthetically. So it seems overzealous to say that they are all the while aesthetic objects. Better to say that they *can* be aesthetic objects—that they have this *potential.* They become aesthetic objects, then, only when they are experienced aesthetically. This sort of definition, of potential and actualization, is a popular conception of what an aesthetic object is. To restate, any object is potentially an aesthetic object; what makes it actually so is for it to be the object of someone's aesthetic experience, that is, that it be actually experienced aesthetically.

This definition, however, does have a couple of apparent problems. First, it would seem that we are allowing the status of the object to change. Second, we are basing this *objective* change in a *subjective* change, that the *object* changes depending on how it is viewed. Subjectivism like this is plagued by the probability that different people will view at different times different objects aesthetically. So this apparently allows for a single object to be both an aesthetic object *and not* an aesthetic object at the same time, if only that two people are viewing it differently.

Some answer this challenge by biting the bullet and declaring every object on earth to be now and forevermore an aesthetic object. This is a hard bullet to bite. No one may ever experience the clump of dust hidden behind an old desk as an aesthetic object, so why give it the exalted status of being an aesthetic object? Another avenue of dealing with this is to explain this *potential-actual* relationship with greater detail. If one were to maintain that the object in question *does not* go through an objective change, then the account might have a chance. To explain: Some contend that an object, to be an aesthetic object, need only have properties that *can* be experienced aesthetically. Since all sensible objects do in fact have properties that can be experienced aesthetically, even that clump of dust, all objects *can* be aesthetic objects. However, it is only when objects are actually being experienced aesthetically that they become or take on the status of being aesthetic objects. The reason for this, it is claimed, is *not a change in the objects themselves.* They have the same properties whether they are or are not being experienced aesthetically. The change is in the *focus* of attention of the viewer. If the viewer looks at the properties of the object and notices only the object's ability to, say, get good gas mileage, then she is not experiencing it aesthetically, and it is not an aesthetic object. If however, she is appreciating the lines, shapes, and colors of the object, then she is focusing on properties of the object that provide a basis for an aesthetic experience, and so the object is an aesthetic one. The object does not change. It has the same properties whether being experienced aesthetically or not. What changes is only the focus of the viewer. "Gas mileage" and "the beauty of this object" are both based on appreciating various features of the object. But the variety of properties present are seen only in focusing on different aspects or different arrangements of those objective properties.

By avoiding a change in status of the object, by putting the onus solely on the viewer for determining the aesthetic status of the object, we treat the label 'aesthetic object' as a *conceptual distinction* rather than as an objective one. We can see this in many other cases, too. One can view the sunset the way the navigator might (since the sun generally sets in the west); one can view it the way the meteorologist might (dark vivid colors perhaps mean rain); one can view it as the astrophysicist might (certain colors are indicative of certain gaseous phenomena); and one can view it as the aesthete might ("My, that's a lovely sunset"). The sunset does not change from view to view (for those in relatively the same viewing position). The only thing that changes is the *focus* of the various viewers. And so it is with aesthetic objects. Just as almost every physical object in the world can be used as some kind of tool, every object in the world is a candidate for being viewed aesthetically, and therefore for being an aesthetic object.

A final question: Is the aesthetic object a *physical* object? Consider the following case. When we view an aesthetic object, we generally make several judgments about which of the properties of the object we will focus on. We may make those decisions based on what type of experience we would like to have in attendance to the object, or we may make those decisions based on dividing up the aesthetic properties of the object from the nonaesthetic ones. In any event, there are generally properties of the object that we ignore in considering the thing as an aesthetic object.

In some theatrical plays there are *Chinese prop men*. These prop handlers do not attempt to conceal themselves from the gaze of the audience (neither do they try to be intrusive). But generally their presence and actions are ignored because they are really not part of the aesthetic object. They are, without question, part of the *object*—they take up space on stage, they move things about, and they are quite visible. But since they do not *directly* involve themselves with the aesthetic quality of the play, or with our aesthetic experience of the play, they are not considered part of the aesthetic object. In short, the aesthetic object is generally different from the physical object. The physical object is generally considered the *vehicle* of the aesthetic object, but the aesthetic object itself is only the perceptual object, and only that part or those aspects of the perceptual object that fit into an aesthetic accounting of the object, that is, increase the value of the object *as* aesthetic, or figure into our aesthetic experience of the object.

CHAPTER 4

Defining "Art"

SECTION ONE: WHY DEFINE "ART"?*

Early in my career I gave a series of lectures on defining 'art'. As is my usual practice, I first tried to offer some reason for why attempting a definition of 'art' is useful. One student, however, was not convinced by my appeal to common sense that *of course* there are objects (and events) in the world that are art and others that are not. She objected that by her lights "art is anything one says it is." Her objection was hardly unusual. And I answered her challenge by pushing my appeal to common sense. I wadded up a sheet of paper, placed it on the lectern, and asked, "Is this art? Can you, should you, consider this the same sort of object as the *Mona Lisa*?" (Sometimes this is enough to silence the objection—either the added strength behind the intuition *or* the intimidation that a teacher can muster in confronting a student individually.) However, in this case the student did not back down but repeated her claim that art is anything one regards as art, *and* one might just as well call the wadded-up paper art as call painted canvasses or snow shovels, urinals, Brillo boxes, or beds art. (I am thinking here, of course, of the works of such artists as Duchamp, Warhol, Rauschenberg, Oldenburg, and others.)

The story is light, but it masks a serious challenge: Why define 'art'? Why, in the face of the overwhelming challenge to definitions of art that (bona fide) art in the last two centuries offers, ought we attempt to limit the set of objects

---

*Portions of this section are taken from "Why Define 'Art'?" *Journal of Aesthetic Education*, 28:1 (Spring 1994), pp. 71–76, and are reprinted here with permission.

and events that we refer to as 'art'? Why not simply allow "whatever one says is art *is* art"?

Suppose we label the position that "an object or event is art if it is regarded as art or labeled 'art' " as the "Nondefinition" in virtue of the motivation of the position to escape any restrictions that definitions of art have traditionally placed on art. One initial move may be to consider the Nondefinition related to those positions that have collectively come to be known as Antiessentialism. The central claims of Antiessentialism seem to be, in principle, two. First, there is no *essence* to art: that is, there is no possibility of articulating a single definition to capture what we take to be art. Second, what definition*s* we may offer must be framed either (1) as a series of *disjuncts* ("art is this *or* that *or* the other thing"), (2) in such a way that some art objects share similarities with other art objects, but there is no feature that they *all* share—the way, say, that no member of a family may share a single feature with every other member of that family, yet each is still a family member, or (3) as open-ended or evolutionary, as capable of change and progression over time (this is taken from the work of Morris Weitz). The difficulty, however, with the Nondefinition is that it shares only in the first of the two claims. Furthermore, it is important to see Antiessentialism as holding the second claim—*or some such positive word on definitions of art*—because without this, Antiessentialism becomes nothing more than the Nondefinition, at least nothing more of interest. Antiessentialism, the view that there is no essential nature to art, at least no *single* essential nature, is not the same as the Nondefinition, and this is because Antiessentialism as a full position about defining 'art' makes some positive claim that restricts to some degree the use of the term 'art'. The Nondefinition makes no claim limiting use of the term 'art'.

I think there are three central arguments against the Nondefinition. The first is the Meaning Argument, the second is the Challenge Argument, and the third is the Criticism Argument.

THE MEANING ARGUMENT

When we use the word 'art', we apparently mean something by it. When we use the word 'art', we refer to, at least, some objects and/or events in the world. But just as importantly, use of the word 'art' entails *not* referring to some objects. That is, the meaning of the word 'art' is not merely positive, in that it picks out objects; the meaning is also negative, in that the word *excludes* reference to some objects. This is the case with nearly every word we use. Few words pick out everything. And 'art' is not one of them. For the word 'art' to be meaningful is for it to *exclude reference to some objects*.

If the word 'art' picks out anything one thinks is art, then there is no object that is not art. This is so because one can—and may—pick out anything and everything as being art. This makes the term meaningless, or it makes the term equal in meaning to the term 'everything.' But 'art' is not a synonym of 'everything', and to treat the word 'art' that way is to not use the word the way users of the English language use the word.

We mean by 'art' something about objects or events. We mean something of these objects that is relatively stable and is about *objects and events* in the world, not about how one may regard them. We mean something that is about *only some* of the objects in the world (so that the crumpled-up paper that I threw away at the end of that class was definitely *not* art). And we mean something that is a bestowal of value on the object. This last point leads to the second argument.

THE CHALLENGE ARGUMENT

The claim that something is *not* art can be a strong claim. Suppose that one day Sam is touring a gallery and sees what appears to be a Brillo pad box on display. In spite of the fact that it has a small plague next to it and in spite of the fact that a recognized artist created that particular object, Sam declares, "*That* is *not* art." This means something—but not just in the sense that the English words go together correctly or communication takes place. When Sam declares that something is not art, he seems to be issuing a strong challenge, meeting what he takes to be *the artist's* strong challenge in having the audacity to place that object in a museum. (Whether the artist *meant* the challenge or not, the challenge is still made in the presentation of the piece.)

One makes a strong critical statement about an object in saying that it is not art. Moreover, this reaction is, in some measure, the sort of response someone like Warhol might have expected. Whether he means to or not, Warhol stretches our collective concept of art, perhaps even stretching our *definition* of art. Were this not possible, why would he place this object in the museum? It is easier to see *in the supermarket* a Brillo pad box. If all that one labels 'art' is art, then why ought not Warhol simply allow Sam to see the box at the market and label it there? What do Brillo boxes mean to him? Of course the point of his creating it and presenting it *as art* is just because we do not as a routine matter see Brillo boxes as art. And this "routine matter" is of course part of what makes Warhol's presentation so evocative.

The Nondefinition either does not allow or cannot explain the interest we take in Warhol's work. If "everything one says is art is art" is correct, then there is no basis for Sam's surprise when he differs with others. The conflict over whether an object presented as art in a gallery or museum really is art is one of depth. Lengthy debates, long critical notices, and heated tempers probably accompanied the first presentations of the works of Duchamp, Rauschenberg, and others. The Nondefinition cannot account for this. If art is anything one says it is, then it is foolish to waste time supporting the claim that something is not art.

Nonetheless, the claim that an object is *not* art is still a powerful one—one that makes us consider the nature of art with some care, one that may even scare us a bit in having to stretch our (apparently) settled concepts. The last section concentrated on the meaning of the word 'art' as exclusionary of some objects. This section focuses on the word 'art' as *inclusive* of some objects. Today's 'art' refers to some objects that might, without the artistic revolutions of the past two centuries, never be viewed as art. The admission to the province of art of work coming out of the Postimpressionist, Abstractionist, Cubist, Dadaist, Modernist, and Postmodernist movements has created some stir. Without a concept, without a definition that could be meaningfully challenged and perhaps eventually broadened, the strength of work from those movements would have been severely lessened. The ability to challenge whatever the current conception of art is, the ability to make the claim "that is not art," would be lost through acceptance of the Nondefinition.

THE CRITICISM ARGUMENT

When Sally judges an art object, she may judge it against a *pre-set standard*. When Sally watches the Miami City Ballet dancers, she may consider whether their work was indeed good ballet—that is, good *as* ballet. She begins with a concept of what ballet essentially is and rates the performance against that concept. Without a concept or definition of ballet, Sally is unable to make these dependent or functional judgments. The Nondefinition allows no evaluations against a standard because Sally may not state what ballet is. Even if the proponent of the Nondefinition allows her to define 'ballet', she may still not judge an object against a conception of 'art'. This, given the Nondefinition, is not an option.

Aristotle defined goodness in functional terms, something along the lines of "X is good if it is a highly functional one of its kind (and the more functional, the better)." Judgments based on this sort of definition of goodness turn on being clear about the relationship of the object in question to others "of its kind." If we cannot define 'art' in stable and meaningful terms, then it is not open to anyone to evaluate some object functionally as art. But, again, a great deal of art criticism today is exactly of that sort: X is a good example of a sonnet; Y is a good interpretation of Beethoven's *Ninth*; Z is good *art*.

When all is said and done, there is good reason to create and consider various definitions of art. The opposite—that art is only "what one says it is"—renders absurd results, such indeed that we are not able to use the word 'art' meaningfully. 'Art', to be meaningful, must be exclusive and inclusive. It must exclude some objects in the world from being art, else the word comes to be a synonym for "everything." It must also include some objects as art, with admission to that group characterized by consideration and *testing*. The Nondefinition cannot function as a definition of art, principally because it leaves meaningfulness out.

SECTION TWO: IMITATION AND REPRESENTATION—THE ANCIENT GREEK VIEW

Of all the questions in aesthetics, *What is art?* is the oldest. Interestingly, the first answer to this question was not something clearly articulated by a single thinker. Rather the first answer to the question was something that was commonly accepted by various societies. For this discussion, the society in question is that of ancient Athens. The people of ancient Athens believed they knew what was meant by 'art'. The common person could express what art was, and so there was no need for further exploration. So, in a sense, the definition with which Plato worked was more *inherited* than invented. Plato, who lived between 428 and 347 B.C., was the first known Western philosopher to consider the nature of art.

Athenians in Plato's day believed that the character of art was *to imitate nature*. This theory, which we can call the Imitation Theory, or the Mimesis Theory, held that art objects are objects that imitate nature. Now, this is not meant to suggest that art was *precision copying* of nature. Nonetheless, works of art all resembled, in simple sensory terms, objects in nature. A statue of a man looked like a man. A painting of a tree looked like a tree. (Of course, a *painting* of a tree probably resembled another painting more than it resembled a tree, and this may be part of the reason that "mimetic" theory evolved into "representation" theory.)

Here the idea of imitation or mimesis is that the art object resembled, or *looked like* (in the case of visual art), whatever it was meant to represent. This is not exactly what is meant by 'representation' nowadays. Today when aestheticians speak of representation they are not necessary speaking of a *resemblance* relationship between the art object and the natural object it represents. The relationship between these two objects may be "symbolic" or "semiotic," where the artwork stands as a *symbol* or a *sign* of the object it represents. However, in ancient Athens, the theory that focused on a *resemblance* relationship was the norm.

Very ancient humans drew pictures on cave walls, pictures that commonly were meant to stand for animals that they were interested in (for food or spiritual purposes, for instance). Primitive works created between thousands-of-years B.C. and hundreds-of-years B.C. commonly imitate some aspect of nature, either of animals, of themselves, or, more sophisticatedly, of beings who represent natural forces, such as gods of rain, harvest, or fertility. Of course, many works that represent other things were not created to simply *look like* those other things. Visual imitation, though perhaps mostly commonly thought of as the paradigm of ancient representation, is not the only sort available. Plato and Aristotle dealt most directly with representation of two sorts: visually imitative (paintings and sculptures) and literarily imitative (poetry and drama).

PLATO

Though Plato and Aristotle did not create the theory they considered, they accepted it as the standard, as the "received view." This is particularly the case with Plato.

Plato had several problems with the received view: that art is essentially imitation. Plato's work is recorded in Book Ten of his *Republic*, in the *Ion*, and in the *Symposium* (and perhaps Books Two and Three of the *Republic* and his *Phaedrus*). In order to understand why he criticized the common view, we first must examine how Plato saw the world and how he viewed the possibility of understanding and gaining knowledge about the world.

Plato describes reality as being composed of two levels, a natural physical level that we experience through our senses and a level beyond our senses consisting of the *essences* of all things. Plato says that sensible objects—objects we sense—"participate" in their essences, and he calls these essences the *Forms* or *Ideas*. Consider an example. Perhaps you are sitting in a chair while reading this. As you look around, perhaps you see other chairs in the room. The question that Plato asked is this: How are all of the chairs in the room—which differ in how they look, how they are constructed, and, most basically, in that they are separate individual chairs—related to one another, such that each is correctly called a 'chair'? It is not that they all have four legs, a seat, and a back; it may be that not all the chairs fulfill this definition. It is not that we can pick them out using the definition "to be sat upon," because one can sit on the floor, on the bed, on the kitchen counter, and none of these items are chairs. Plato determined that what made each object that is correctly called a 'chair' a chair is not the way it looks (etc.), but that it shares in a single essence, the essence of what it is to be a chair.

An important aspect of Plato's motivation in theorizing that there exists more than just the natural, physical level comes through his treatment of knowledge, of how we come to know what we know. Plato believed that the only way we can know is for the object of our knowledge to be *permanent*. To know something is to know something that is stable and unchanging. The physical world, the one where there are individual physical objects, is constantly changing. So, he inferred, there must be a world where the objects of knowledge are fixed and unchanging. This world, the Heaven of Ideas, contains the essences of objects of knowledge. And essences do not change. If we really know about chairs, we know about the essence of what it is to be a chair.

There are, of course, apparent problems that philosophers find with a theory like Plato's. In fact, he brings up many of the problems himself in his dialogue *Parmenides*. For Plato's treatment of art to be correct is not for his "two-level reality" theory to be correct—and neither the reverse. However, in order to understand Plato's treatment of art and what motivates him to create it, one must first understand his two-level reality theory and how it provides a means for us to know what is constant and immutable about the world.

The received view of art, for Plato, is that art is imitation. For an object to be an art object is for it to

(1) be an artifact, and

(2) be an imitation of some object in the natural world.

Plato took this to be the standard view, with his task being one of *considering* or criticizing this view. Here, any work created either with the intention of being viewed as an imitation of something in the natural world, or actually being viewed that way, constitutes an art object. In Athens, Plato saw that statues of warriors, of gods, and of young men shared a goal: to come as close to a good copy as possible, while at the same time to incorporate certain stylistic conventions that made ordinary and art objects somewhat visually different. At heart, though, art objects were simply imitations of objects that existed in nature.

The artist—in creating an imitation of some natural object—is in fact creating an imitation *of an imitation*, if we think, as Plato did, of natural objects as *imitations* of the *Forms* or *Ideas*. Such removal from reality, from the essences of things, prompted Plato to question the value of art. Art, says Plato, suffers because it is removed from stable and permanent reality. Natural objects are imitations of essences. Art, then, consists of imitations of imitations. Art, instead of bringing us closer to reality, pushes us away. In art there is no reality, no possibility of knowledge. An understanding or even appreciation of true beauty does not come from an appreciation of art objects. A true appreciation of beauty comes from seeing the structure of this world, then seeing the elegance of abstract concepts like mathematics, then contemplating the essential Forms, and finally contemplating the Form of the Good and the Form of Beauty (this is explored in the *Symposium*).

Plato's task, as he saw it, was not to describe the nature of art. Instead, the task was to consider the common view, as illustrated in the artforms and artworks he saw around him, and *to question its value*. Imitative art provides no lasting knowledge, and, so far as the chief goal of humans is attainment of knowledge of the truth, art serves contrary purposes. If art has a value, it is the power to strengthen the relationship between the citizenry and the state. Essentially, if art has value, its value is patriotic or as propaganda. (We will explore this topic later in the chapter on censorship, chapter 7.)

ARISTOTLE

Aristotle's writings about art have a markedly different tone from Plato's, although the two discussed the same sorts of things. The received view for

Aristotle, as for Plato, was that art is imitation of nature. However, for Aristotle, art-as-imitation is *not* negative. A basis for the difference in their respective attitudes can be found in their rather different approaches to understanding the world. Plato thinks we must constantly strive to leave our consideration of natural-worldly things for contemplation of the Forms. But Aristotle denied the existence of a Heaven of Ideas, or Forms that exist separate from the actual physical objects of which they are the essences. For Aristotle, reality consists solely of the natural world that we sense, the world of many chairs and many tables, and so forth.

Part of what Aristotle took to be natural was imitation. Imitation is natural to animals, and particularly to animals of higher intelligence, such as primates. This is particularly true of humans. Not only is it natural to imitate nature, but it is natural to be *delighted*, or amused and interested, by imitations of nature. When Sam visits a gallery and considers an artwork that appears imitative, he enjoys noting the similarities and resemblances between that object—or the presentation or image of that object—and the natural object it represents. Art is founded, then, on these two propositions. In an initial Aristotelian analysis, for an object to be an art object is for it to

(1) be an artifact,

(2) be an imitation of nature, and

(3) be delightful to viewers (hearers, etc.).

In Athens, Plato saw statues imitating good examples of warriors, gods, and young men. Instead of focusing on the "imitation," Aristotle focuses on the *"good examples"* aspect. For Plato, the artist simply imitates nature; for Aristotle, the artist does not *simply* imitate nature—she looks to the universal or archetypal in nature. She paints, sculpts, or creates works that celebrate the best of nature, so her work is better, aesthetically, than the originals. Art, then, is not valueless. It is valuable in that it seeks to demonstrate what is good, or best, in nature. So the final version of the Aristotelian definition is: for an object to be an art object is for it to

(1) be an artifact,

(2) be an imitation of *the universal or archetypal* in nature, and

(3) be delightful to viewers (hearers, etc.).

This sort of view takes the mimesis or imitation view of art, essentially the same as the view Plato considered, but describes it in a positive light. Art as it was practiced in ancient times has value, and its value lies in showing us what is best in nature and in delighting us in this representation. By considering a characterization of what is best in a kind of natural object, we can understand, we can *know*, that natural object—or kind of natural object—better.

MIMETIC THEORY CONSIDERED

Since imitation, and later a more sophisticated representationalism, continued in art as the norm throughout the Middle Ages, through the Renaissance, and almost up to the advent of the artistic movement of Impressionism, the Representation Theory of Art also persisted, though declining in popularity after the Renaissance. Of course, with the beginning of Impressionism, and then of Postimpressionism, the Mimetic and Representational Theories of Art lost much of their following.

Part of evaluating whether a theory is viable is to determine how *strong* a reading we wish to apply to the definition. If what is meant by saying that "art is imitation" is that it is necessary and sufficient for an art object to *copy* some object in nature, then we might well say that the theory was shown to be untenable as early as the advent of representational Egyptian art, with its odd poses and elongated eyes. If we mean that an art object represents in a way where we see that the object *stands for* some natural object in a direct sense, then we can adopt this theory *up to* the time when artists give up a standard of "realism in representation" or imitation. Once one sees the work of Monet and Picasso as art, one has a more difficult time adopting a purely imitative theory of art, given that the intents of the artists are no longer to represent in any straightforward way.

However, one may elect to take a more modest reading of "representational" so that if objects simply represent some aspect of the world, no matter how abstractly, then that is enough for an object to be art. This sort of reading treats the notion of "representation" more in line with the way the term is used today. Today 'representation' need not mean anything like "copying." Representation may simply mean "standing for" in a direct, nonsymbolic way. The problem is that even here we may find counterexamples: Many art objects today show only form or structure, with no representational content. Consider purely formalized music or purely formalized paintings, such as those of Postmodernism.

Another problem with the Representation Theory is that an object might well represent a thing in more than one way, or it might represent different things to different viewers. Although it would be odd to think of a cloud as an art object, it is easy for us to think of a cloud as a representative object. In viewing a cloud, Sam sees a dragon breathing fire. Sally sees a bee alighting on a flower. For the Representational Theory to work, does the viewer have to see the object represented the same way the artist did? Or the same way that all other viewers do? Again, what if Sally sees a bee-and-flower at one viewing, but sees the dragon at another? Does there need to be a single object that is represented through the art object? Perhaps these problems can be addressed, but it is not obvious that they can be handled without adding more to the theory.

The problems with a hard reading of the Representation Theory of Art are obvious; the problems with a softer reading are equally obvious. None of this is meant to suggest that the Representational Theory of Art—either in its ancient imitative guise or in more contemporary formulations—is untenable.

Indeed, in each consideration of each theory, there will appear some difficulties, no matter how minor. The point in doing this is not to advocate skepticism, nor to convince the student of aesthetics that this is a fruitless task. The point is merely to show that every theory has its proponents and its detractors, every theory has problems, and the fun of philosophizing about theories is in attempting to work out the bugs of whichever theory is most attractive. The key for the reader of aesthetics, then, is to either find a theory whose problems are not overwhelmingly damaging to the view or to find a theory worth saving and begin to address and answer the difficulties.

SECTION THREE: ROMANTICISM

Chronologically, the second theory to attempt a definition of art is the Romantic Theory. Romanticism followed the Enlightenment, that point where the Middle Ages, informed by religion and authority, gave way to a celebration of the abilities of individuals and their particular reasoning skills. Strangely enough, Romanticism was anti-Enlightenment in a strong sense. While the Enlightenment promoted intellectual endeavors, Romanticism focused on *the passionate or emotional*. Romanticism was interested in the *state* of the individual, emotionally and introspectively. And so Romanticism saw art as essentially the outpouring of the individual's passionate nature, of personal feelings.

This is not to say that artists were simply creating vehicles of self-emotional expression. Their works, on some views, were intended to *communicate* these feelings. On some views, the feelings were meant to be essentially universal. On some views, these works acted as *symbols* of these universal feelings. This communication and sharing of symbols took on a value all its own, and it is in Romanticism that the slogan "art for art's sake" took on its full flower. Art became of extreme importance, not for any instrumental value—not because it *led* to some other value—but for a value all its own. Our first Romantic is the German metaphysician Schopenhauer, who we met previously in discussion of the aesthetic attitude.

ARTHUR SCHOPENHAUER

Arthur Schopenhauer found art not only to be intrinsically valuable, or valuable for itself or on its own, but to be instrumentally valuable as well. In fact, he thought the instrumental value of art was of primary importance; art possessed an instrumental value of the highest order. For Schopenhauer, it is through art that one finds a way to escape the *Will*. To make this clear, we must, as with Plato, understand Schopenhauer's metaphysics.

Like Plato, Schopenhauer believed that the world that we sense is only one part of reality. There is a greater reality, and he described it in a way similar to Plato. Schopenhauer believed in the Platonic Forms. The world that we see, feel, and hear is but a mirror of reality. Unlike Plato, Schopenhauer explained why we are not in direct contact with reality. The problem is that the natural world is absolutely infested with what Schopenhauer called the "Will."

In the *World as Will and Idea*, we read that Will is what characterizes the natural world. The Will is the *will-to-live*; it is desire for the necessities and comforts of survival. Although the Will itself is unknowable, it manifests itself in all want, deficiency, and suffering. It objectifies itself in every action we take, for every action is geared toward our own survival and satisfaction. The irony is that we can never be satisfied. In the natural world, the norm is "want" and the more we attempt to evade "want," the less we are able to do so. To struggle is to reinforce the Will as the harbinger of unhappiness and strife in our lives.

Schopenhauer's metaphysics is not, however, hopeless. Like Plato, Schopenhauer makes provision for gaining access to the world of Forms, which is the world of freedom. He identifies two ways. The first way, the most drastic, is to deliberately deny desire, to become an ascetic and cease the struggle for gain. Tied into this is the admonition to take up philosophy, to focus on contemplation to the exclusion of bodily desire. The second way of escape from the Will is not as permanent as that of the ascetic. Schopenhauer tells us that if we focus on the artistic, and do so in a way that is devoid of will, we can escape the Will. What we must do, then, is contemplate art, especially the universal and essential in art. In doing this, we free ourselves from earthly capture.

The Forms are illustrated or offered to some degree in art objects. The greater the art and the greater the *genius* of the artist, the greater the Forms that will be present in the art. Art objects incorporate elements or facets that are universal. Through art, we are able to rise above the 'particular' and contemplate the Forms. In art, we are presented with the "permanent essential forms of the world and all its phenomena." Since the Idea or Form is extranatural, it releases us and takes us to pure "Will-lessness" where we lose individuality and the pain that comes from desire. This Will-less contemplation of aesthetic objects is characterized by disinterest. Disinterest is practiced by the person of imagination, which Schopenhauer calls the person of artistic genius. It takes artistic genius to create works of art, but it also takes artistic genius to appreciate art objects. Everyone, so far as she is capable of appreciating art, has some degree of this genius, but we all have it in differing degrees. All have some degree of genius in them, in order to appreciate art at all, but most do not have enough to produce art.

Art, then, is the only consolation life offers, apart from adopting the life of an ascetic, to ease the burden of the Will. For an object to be an art object is for it to

(1) be an artifact,

(2) be to some degree an instantiation of the universality and Will-lessness of the Forms, and

(3) be an escape, through contemplation, from the Will.

Now, though this may sound somewhat esoteric, it is not difficult to see this analysis in light of Romanticism. What Schopenhauer suggests, regardless of whether we accept or reject his double-reality theory, is that art is what allows us to escape the unpleasantness of life. We escape by appreciating the universal, the timelessness, the cessation of want and hurt, in art objects.

For Schopenhauer, it is through music, specifically *formal* music, that we are best given the opportunity for escape. Contemplation of formal music, like that of Bach, goes directly to the heart of things. When we appreciate art, we view it disinterestedly, divorcing ourselves from our personal interests and desires. In doing this, we may enjoy the art for its own sake, not as fulfillment of some desire we harbor, but as a means of experiencing what is truly real.

FRIEDRICH NIETZSCHE

It is not difficult to draw a correlation between Romanticism and metaphysical theorizing, especially given Schopenhauer and our next philosopher, Friedrich Nietzsche. Like Schopenhauer, Nietzsche had a concept of Will. But unlike Schopenhauer, Nietzsche's Will is not a negative, pessimistic force. Nietzsche's Will is full of life, creativity, and power.

Nietzsche conceives of art as synthesis of two separate *energies*. These energies burst forth from nature. They are the Apollonian and the Dionysian. Nietzsche calls Apollo the god of all "plastic energies." Apollo represents artifactuality, individuation, labor, structure, and symmetry. Dionysus, on the other hand, represents the antithesis of Apollo. Dionysus represents the death of individuation and structure; he represents freedom of expression, revelry, excitement, spontaneity, liveliness, and perhaps even recklessness. It is through the reconciliation of these two energies, the one toward form, the other toward expression, that the best art is created. This reconciliation happens through the artist and his creative processes.

Tragedy—Nietzsche's most discussed art form—arises, as with the best art, through this synthesis of the Apollonian and Dionysian forces. Tragic art, through an imposition of structure that Nietzsche calls the "Apollonianization of the Dionysian," makes us aware of and able to cope with the harshness of reality. In this way we can understand the world. Tragedy exists not to depress us, not to make us resign ourselves to the negative in life. Tragedy exists to help us affirm life, with all its pain.

Once art is created, it takes on great value. Art, says Nietzsche, makes life possible and worth living. Art is integrally bound up with life. Impulses to create and appreciate art are not only natural, but also *essentially* natural. They lie at the heart of the good life. Art is not merely imitation of nature. It acts as a complement to reality, finishing up where nature leaves off. Art overcomes and transforms. It is anything but stagnant; it is active, not passive or static.

For Nietzsche, then, for an object to be an art object is for it to

(1) be an artifact,

(2) be a creation coming out of the forces of both the Apollonian and the Dionysian, that is, having both the qualities of order/form and life-embracement/ recklessness, and

(3) be a means for us to understand and appreciate life and the rest of nature, to be an affirmation of power, creativity, and fulfillment.

As with Schopenhauer, Nietzsche's definition at first might seem too esoteric to be of practical value. However, once again, it is easy enough to see the call to Romanticism in his definition. We must embrace life and all its pleasure and pain in order to truly live. We have to feel deeply in order to appreciate living. And art affords us this opportunity, not in random fashion, but through order and with the *function* of enhancing life.

One of the things that may continually draw us back to art galleries and theaters is our strong emotional response to certain art objects. This emotional reaction has nearly always been considered an integral part of the art experience. Without it, we are not fully expressing our experience of art, nor are we fully explaining what keeps us going back to the galleries and theaters. Consider your own case. What are the best art experiences that you have ever had? Do you recall them fondly? Do you recall the feelings you had at the time, and perhaps have now in recalling the experience? Many of the most aesthetic experiences, the best experiences of art, have a distinctly strong emotional content. Romanticism cannot, as a theory of art, be dismissed quickly. To do so may be to deny our real-life experience of at least the best art.

ROMANTICISM CONSIDERED

Romanticism is an inspiring tradition, and one that affords us a robustly sensuous understanding of the nature of art. It is broad enough to let us see imitative art as imitating the good in life and nature, of seeing the artistic movements of Impressionism, Expressionism, Realism, and so forth as presentations of deep universal emotions. It even allows us to see works that focus on *form* as rising *through* emotion, as is the case in Schopenhauer's treatment of formal music. It would seem then that emotion can be found in almost any art object, and the expression of that emotion, particularly in a life-affirming way in which we can understand and come to terms with pain and want, is what essentially constitutes art.

The Theory of Romanticism is, though, not without some apparent difficulties. Particularly acute is the problem of the *sufficiency* of a Romantic analysis of art. If art is essentially the vital expression of emotion, is it that all vital expression of emotion is art? What about the fervor of political speakers or spirited preachers? Certainly their activities can be seen as expressive of deep and forceful emotion. Are these activities art? It would, it seems, be the novice who mistakes a political speech or a church sermon for a work of performance art. This is not to say that speeches and sermons cannot be viewed this way, or that a performance-art production could not include a speech or a sermon. But it would be inappropriate to think of the standard Sunday morning church sermon or the president's State of the Union address as a production of art.

Beyond the sufficiency-condition problem, there may be a problem with the *necessity* condition: that all art must contain some expression of emotion. The problem seems to be a species of a larger problem: the problem of artist intention. Though surely the artist can and probably does know her intention regarding a given art creation—barring, say, unconscious reasons for creating certain works—and though she can communicate this to others who wish to criticize or interpret or merely appreciate her work, the artist's intention often cannot be readily discovered. Although one can be reasonably certain of, say, Michelangelo's intention regarding the creation of the *Pietà*, a casual viewer at New York's Museum of Modern Art may be hard pressed to explain the intention behind any *one* of the works of, say, Jackson Pollock. This is because there are certain conventions, common in representational artforms, that allow us to fathom the artist's intentions in the object she created. However, in formalized works or works of profound abstraction, such as Pollock's, the range of suggestion as to his intention in creating a given work may be quite broad.

The artist's intention is frequently invoked in order to either interpret a work or to establish it as a work of art. However, if there is a problem with the invocation of artist intention, given the distance at which we may find ourselves from that intention, then it would seem a bad choice to relegate an object's status as art to the *speculation* that the creator *wished* for a given object to be viewed as art, as well as to the speculation that the object one now refers to as art is indeed the expression of vital emotion.

The difficulty is a simple one. How is it that we can know that a work contains or is an expression of emotion? This may be obvious in many works. But this is a more difficult task when it comes to formalized or highly abstract works. If one is relegated to having to fathom the intention of the artist in order to determine whether the work is an expression of emotion, one may find oneself silent. This is especially true, again, with very formal or abstract works.

SECTION FOUR: EXPRESSIONISM

It will be initially difficult to state clearly the difference between Expressionism as a theory of art and Romanticism as a theory of art. Instead of stipulating a difference that might seem arbitrary, we will simply explore the Theory of Expressionism as a more recent version of the essential element of Romanticism: expression of vital emotion. The only real difference that seems noteworthy at this stage is that the Expressionists are much more concerned with the *communication* of emotions to the viewers. This may indicate that they are less metaphysically inclined and more specific about the mechanics of expressing vital emotion than were the Romantics.

Perhaps a bridge between Romanticism and Expressionism, as chronologically distinct versions of emotion-inducing or "arousal" theories, are the famous words of Wordsworth, that all good poetry is the spontaneous overflow of powerful feelings. The philosophers we will discuss in this section are Leo Tolstoy, a Russian novelist; Benedetto Croce, an Italian Idealist; and R. G. Collingwood, a British philosopher. We will begin with Tolstoy.

LEO TOLSTOY

Leo Tolstoy, no doubt most famous as a novelist, was also an influential and fairly controversial aesthetician. Tolstoy envisioned art as essentially *a form of communication*. Art is meant to communicate *universal emotion*, which is felt by the artist and is the subject of her work, and is then communicated to her audience. Without this communication, the expression of emotion through art is incomplete. Without an audience that reconstructs the emotions of the artist through the medium of her creation, there is no art.

This is very important. Art is not, for Tolstoy, simply the "spontaneous overflow of emotion." Without some connection being made to the viewers or hearers of the art, the artwork is unsuccessful. Mere expression of emotion, just an outpouring of the emotion or of the articulation of the emotion of the artist, is insufficient. Without communication, there is no art—or at the very least no good art. In a sense, Tolstoy is capturing what many of us, in our normal experiences of art, take to be crucial to art: that we—*we* the audience—feel the passion of the art. It is not enough for the artist to have felt something and produced some artifact resulting from that feeling. What has to take place, for the art to be successful, is for us to feel what the artist felt, or at least for us to feel what the artist's work can make us feel. Emotion is important to art. But the communication of that emotion, so that the audience member may feel it, is of paramount importance. The rantings and ravings of an artist, if there is no communication, can result in just so many big messes (say paint thrown wildly onto canvasses, music composed recklessly). While some of the most emotionally communicative art may well have a reckless or random quality, without that recklessness or randomness communicating *to the viewer* the artist's emotion, it is so many big messes.

It is of some importance to note that Tolstoy did *not* believe that art, or the viewing of art, was supposed to impart pleasure to viewers. Instead, art is treated as a natural part of life, not incidental to living, as the accidental feeling of pleasure might be, but a part of life absolutely vital and integral. Art is *not* about pleasure, not even about the pleasure that might be the subject of the artist-audience communication. Art is about the relationship *itself* of artist to audience. Every work of art causes the viewer to enter into a special relationship with the artist, and not only with the artist, but also with everyone else who has at one time or other entered into that same relationship. The "artistic relationship" between artist and audience builds a community of creator, of object, and of all those who experience the object. Without the ability of one person to empathize with the artist, and without the ability of the members of the audience to share in this experience—though they may never meet—art could not exist.

The artist's job is to evoke in herself some feeling once experienced, and then to communicate it to her audience through some sensual medium, through colors, shapes, melodies, harmonies, figures, movements, and so on. Through the externalities of the medium, the artist transfers her feelings to others. The artist seeks to *infect* her audience with these feelings.

Tolstoy, in his *What Is Art?*, writes that "the degree of infectiousness is the sole measure of excellence in art." The stronger the infectiousness, the better the art. And this infectiousness translates to how intensely the viewer experiences the artist's emotion, how clearly she feels it, and how sincere it is. Indeed, it is in the measure of the sincerity that the bulk of the evaluation lies. Important in Tolstoy's exploration of the communication relationship between artist and audience is the *sincerity* with which the artist imbues the work *and* the level of sincerity of the emotions that are raised in the viewers. The artist must never attempt to manipulate her audience. Without a *real* feeling from which the work is created, no art is made.

Beyond the level of communication and the level of sincerity in the infectiousness, says Tolstoy, the artist must also impart to her audience a true sense of the religious attitudes of the society. She must communicate not only feelings, but also those feelings as they accord with the religious context in which the work is made. To create a work that celebrates cowardice or faithlessness would, it seems, be anathema in any society. To create a work that celebrates resolve, courage, strength, and order is to create in the best tradition of the Greeks. To create a work that celebrates compassion, spirituality, love, and hope is to create a work that fits well into the religious environment of strongly Judeo-Christian societies.

The requirements, then, that are placed on the artist by Tolstoy are rather numerous and even arduous. For an object to be a work of art is for it to

(1) be an artifact,

(2) be an infectious form of communication of sincerely felt universal emotion,

(3) invoke sincere feeling in its audience, and

(4) accord with the religious environment in which it is created.

Problems with Tolstoy's definition might be immediately apparent and may cloud one from seeing the good in his account. Some of the initial problems unique to Tolstoy's conception of Art as Expression are the following: First, it is a common ingredient in much art, especially lately, that instead of supporting the religious climate, that it *challenges* this climate. If we dismissed objects that purport to be art on the grounds that they do not accord religiously with the societal environment, then a number of objects that we all apparently correctly refer to as art would not be. This is the most obvious problem.

A second problem unique to Tolstoy is the infectiousness of *actual* feeling. Although the condition of communicating emotion is standard to the tradition of Expressionism, the edict to *infect* the audience with a *sincere* level of the feeling being expressed may be excessive. What if we see a painting celebrating martyrdom, perhaps St. Sebastian's. Should we feel the stings of the arrows along with the saint? Should we feel the bondage, the physical agony, and so forth? Is to feel *sincerely* to feel the emotion *completely* or merely in an abstract way?

Should we feel as if we ought to attempt to stop the pain? What about in the case of the murder of Duncan by MacBeth? Should we, in thoroughly feeling what is happening on stage, try to dissuade MacBeth from his treachery or try to wrestle the knife away from him? This level of audience empathy seems excessive and out of character when it comes to the proper reaction to artworks. While Tolstoy would not have us rushing onto stage or empathetically bleeding at the consideration of the predicament of St. Sebastian, to understand just what an infection of sincere emotion is creates questions.

Perhaps the answer to the question is that we should not feel as St. Sebastian did, but we should feel as the *artist* felt as she contemplated the situation of St. Sebastian. If this is the appropriate response, then we may be met with a similar problem to one discussed in the last section, one of understanding or *accessing* artist intentions or artist emotions. But this is not a problem unique to Tolstoy or to the interpretation directly above.

BENEDETTO CROCE

Benedetto Croce, an Italian Idealist who lived toward the end of the 19th century and halfway through the 20th, was also a subscriber to the Expression Theory of Art. Unlike Tolstoy and a bit more like the Romantics, Croce was not so much concerned with details like sincerity, infectiousness, and religious climate as he was with an investigation of the mechanics of expression itself. How does an artist express through artistic creation? What does she express?

'Feeling' was much too ambiguous a term for Croce. Art could not be a matter of mere expression of emotions. What were expressed were not feelings but *intuitions*, and more specifically, *lyrical* intuitions. Here we see a rather pointed break between the Romantics and the 20th-century Expressionist. The interest is not in merely the passionate side, but is returning, as in the Enlightenment, to the cognitive faculties of human beings.

For Croce, aesthetics is the science of images or intuitive knowledge. We are told that aesthetic experience is one form of cognitive experience. When we are conscious of the world, we are first conscious of what Croce calls "raw sense impressions." When we clarify these, they become intuitions. These intuitions are the building blocks of artistic expression. To express these intuitions successfully is to create art. Unsuccessful art is not a fault of the expression of the intuition. Rather, the failure is due to the intuition's not having been developed fully from the sense impression.

Art is, says Croce, intuition. But by 'intuition' he does not mean an instinctual knowing, as the word may be commonly used today, or a grasp of self-evident truth, as philosophers like Descartes may mean by the word. 'Intuition' is rather an inner vision of an image. It is an immediate knowledge through the contemplation of that image by the imagination of the perceiver. It is the most basic and most fundamental operation of mental activity.

Since art is so closely tied to the expression of intuition, it follows that the work of art per se is *not* the physical object, but the *expressed intuition itself.* The work of art is not a physical thing, but a mental re-creation. The physical work is merely a medium of communication, merely the vehicle of transmitting the expression. On the other hand, the artwork is not something supersensible, occupying, say, some Platonic realm. Instead, Croce tells us that the artwork is the conscious consideration "in all its concreteness." This is to say that the artwork is the deliberate contemplation of an image of something, with the image being contemplated in its most basic form. Moreover, the intuition could not be expressed in any way *other* than through the artist's creation. It is ineffable. The expression of *that* intuition *could* exist only through that particular art work expressing it.

Pure imitation is not art. It may be respectable or admirable, Croce says, but it is not art. Simple representation does not express the clear intuition that Croce makes his touchstone. The artist must, in a very robust sense, think about, "will," and "act" on the intuition to adequately express it. The artist must explore and mull over the image to clarify the intuition before expression. Imitation of some object in nature does not require this cognitive activity. And so imitation per se is not art. This would include imitation of natural objects, and it also serves as an answer to why *original* art objects are themselves so much more interesting and more valuable than copies of those originals.

Part of the need for this "mulling over" before expression is that a necessary ingredient of art is the human personality. Moreover, Croce says, human personality finds its completion in morality. This makes another necessary ingredient of art a moral consciousness. This is reminiscent of Tolstoy, though Croce does not dictate *which* moral consciousness (and he does not mention religion). Perhaps Croce meant, as Tolstoy may have, that art should support the general moral tone of the society. Or perhaps Croce meant that art should express the *artist's* moral sense.

Whichever he meant, Croce, like Tolstoy, encounters problems on this issue. There exist many works that not only communicate no moral consciousness, but about which it is also unlikely that the artist had any intention of expressing anything moral. What is the moral consciousness found in, say, the later work of Pollock, or in the work of Braque? Though they may, with some effort, be seen to be making statements about some aspect of the world or society, it is difficult to find anything particularly or specifically moral in their work.

Croce's analysis, minus the moral consciousness condition, is the following: for an object to be an art object is for it to

(1) be an artifact, and
(2) be an expression of an artist's intuition, with that intuition being clarified and explored on the artist's part.

Croce seems to be ahead of his time, at least with regard to the shift from the emotional as the basis of artistic expression to the cognitive or intellectual. Given the nature of 20th-century art, there is clear reason to shift from the passionate and sentimental to cognition and rationality. Twentieth-century art, just after Abstract Expressionism, is less for the heart and more for the mind. By that of course is meant that art took on a distinctively conceptual tenor. Instead of feeling what the artist intended or what the art object communicated, much 20th-century work is to be thought about. What does the artist *mean*? What challenges does this work present? How is this work best interpreted? The way we consider art after Abstract Expressionism is much more cognitive than perhaps it ever was before. No longer is the advice to feel something in the face of the art object; now we are called upon to *think something*. The role of the audience, the receiver, is not lessened per se. It is simply altered. Instead of feeling, now we think.

Much of 20th-century art—what we haphazardly and all-inclusively call 'Modern' and 'Postmodern' Art—requires a greater commitment to consideration and mulling over than art of a more emotional or even representational nature. People would rather be delighted than called upon to ruminate pensively. And much of Modern Art does not so straightforwardly delight. The key may be one of *investment*. If one is willing to invest time and energy in thinking about the Modern Art object—considering what it means or how it can be interpreted, or even how it fits into the history of art and what challenges it presents—perhaps one will be rewarded with a deeper understanding, a deeper appreciation, a deeper *delight* than might otherwise be the case through the immediately emotional work of times prior to the 20th century. In any event, Benedetto Croce was a man interested in the cognitive formation of the ideas, or intuitions, that are expressed in art, and this is certainly closer to what the contemporary viewer of contemporary art is called upon to do than analyses that are *simply* emotional.

R. G. COLLINGWOOD

Following rather closely behind Croce is the English philosopher, Robin G. Collingwood. Collingwood's theory is expressed (forgive the pun) in his book *The Principles of Art.* It is less theoretic in tone than Croce's theory of art as expression. Collingwood begins his analysis with an attempt to define 'art' as a word that is used in common speech. In his book, he explores how the word, and concept, 'art' has been used. He discusses its connection with "craft," with "representation," with "magic," and with "amusement." The first use of the word, Collingwood tells us, is to signify "skill" or "craft." We still use 'art' today to mean this. One talks about the "art of teaching" or the "art of motorcycle maintenance." But this is not what Collingwood calls "art proper." The ancient Greeks, as we have explored, used the term art to signify "representation" or "imitation." This definition is not far from the previous one of 'craft'. In representation the artist must exercise great skill in producing some object that represents, that is, is *seen* to represent, some natural object. Even today we take drawing classes and painting classes, probably not to learn to be creative or novel, but to learn the *technique(s)* of skillful art creation. We learn about shadows, dimensions, negative space, and all manner of other things. This of course is to learn certain skills. So the ancient Greek notion of art as representation was not very dissimilar from the notion of 'craft'. The imitative works that Plato and Aristotle considered were conceived in the same way as other skills or crafts. Next in Collingwood's study, the Latin word "ars" meant any kind of learning that could be acquired from books or acquired discursively. It was not until the late 18th century that a distinction regarding art included "the fine arts" or "the beautiful arts." In his study, Collingwood determines that (1) art, or *art proper,* has something to do with making things, and (2) art proper has something to do with arousing emotion, though it is not, he hastens to add, synonymous with it. Collingwood then proceeds with his Expressionist analysis.

First, he agrees with Croce that it is naive to say that an artist merely expresses emotion. Collingwood sees the expression of emotion as having definite elements, some of the necessary ones being (1) that the emotion is not simply mentioned to the audience, but is *demonstrated* to them; (2) the emotion is individualized, is this emotion *here and now,* not just one of a species, say, of happiness or sadness; and (3) the expression is not simply for the arousal of emotion, for the expression of emotion that is art is not *manipulative.* The artist must be absolutely candid with his audience. Without complete honesty on the part of the artist, the expression can be nothing other than merely manipulative, or, worse, simply without feeling. On the other hand, the artist must handle the emotion she is expressing delicately. She must not rant and rave (Collingwood accused Beethoven of this). She must not preach, but must gently and subtly communicate a specific, unique emotion.

So, for an object to be an art object is for it to

(1) be an artifact (specifically mentioned in Collingwood's analysis), and

(2) be the careful and candid expression of some particular emotion in a unique manner.

Besides giving us a refined view of art as emotional expression, Collingwood provides us with a view of contemporary philosophy, too. The turn to language—the careful study of terms and how they go together, what they refer to, and what we think of when we use them—is a hallmark of much 20th-century philosophy. Collingwood, who engages in this sort of language analysis, takes us still further in the quest for answers to our traditional questions. With Croce we have perhaps a move in the subject matter, from the purely emotional to the cognitive. With Collingwood we have a move in the manner in which the questions are handled.

EXPRESSIONISM CONSIDERED

For most readers, the Expression Theory of Art that Collingwood describes is the one most familiar and perhaps most palatable. This Expressionism is not weighed down with either a religious/moral commitment nor with a heavy metaphysical commitment. Furthermore, it does not have the obvious defect of the art work being a mere outpouring of emotion, like some primordial scream. Emotion has always played a key role in the appreciation of art for many viewers, and indeed, a strong case can be made for saying that some affective motivation is necessary for us to experience art as art. (Note that a definition of what constitutes art *based solely on our appreciation* of a work as art is a different theory than the Expressionism with which we are dealing here.) An Expressionist theory typically does not focus on the receptivity of the audience; it focuses on the artist and the processes of creation. However, for the expression in the art to be fully successful, the audience and the communication of artist to audience seems a necessary ingredient. The best artists will produce works out of a construction of emotion in some artistic medium, and will produce them so that they do communicate to us, so that they *touch* us. The Expressionist theory might best be seen, then, as a sort of relationship theory of artists-expressing-and-communicating and audiences-feeling-in-response.

In any case, there are still some apparent problems with an Expressionist theory. The first is the possibility of true communication. It may be the case that in all communicatory or relational definitions of art, where the audience needs to understand what it is that is being communicated or expressed to them, that we cannot accurately or even adequately be sure we are correct. If this is indeed problematic, then we are without a means of *knowing* whether or not we are being communicated to effectively. Are we getting the right message? And it would seem that the success of the expression is key to determining (1) whether the art is good art, and (2) more basically, whether it is even art at all. It is this second consideration that ought to worry us; if we are *accidentally* communicated to, without the necessary steps being taken by the artist, then the work, no matter how artistic we judge it to be, is not art. So the question "Is it important for us to get the right message?" seems, for an Expression Theorist, still important.

Another apparent problem with the re-creation of what the artist wishes to express is the following: what about those cases where the artist really *does not know* what she is attempting to express? There are Freudian and other psychological critics who suggest that the artist may not be fully in conscious touch with what actually does get expressed through the art work. Perhaps one may be willing to acquiesce, saying that it does not matter whether the artist is fully and consciously in touch with the emotion or intuition that is being expressed, so long as there is adequate and honest expression. This is plausible, though it suffers from the fact that no one, not even the artist herself, then is in a position to know what actually is being expressed.

But finally, what about the work of art that seems to reveal no expression of emotion whatever? And what if we complicate the story by adding the fact that the artist did not intend to express any emotion? If there are indeed art objects that (1) were not intended to express emotion, and (2) do not in fact communicate any emotion, then it seems that an Expression Theory of Art is not complete. This, perhaps the most difficult point of all, is alluded to in passing with Croce's theory. Perhaps the idea of expression of *emotion* is too simple.

Consider the problem with purely formalized music. And consider some of the computerized creations of music of the past couple of decades. Here the computer is programmed to generate certain mathematical equations correlated with sounds. As the computer generates various values, various sounds are produced. Since the math instantiates certain patterns, so does the music. In a sense, this is not drastically different from the highly formalized way in which Baroque composers used counterpoint and other musical/mathematical techniques for generating sound patterns. Computerized music, while interesting as music and as valid a candidate for being called "music" as other formalized compositions, is essentially no expression of emotion. One can see the problem in stark relief in consideration of visual art produced in the 20th century. No longer is the call to feel in many cases; now the call on the audience is to *think*. Perhaps the idea of expression is still appropriate, but the idea of simply expressing emotion may be too simplistic.

The Expressionist Theory has been adopted widely, not just by aestheticians, critics, and artists. The Expression Theory, then, may be seen as offering us challenges, too, just as art itself does.

SECTION FIVE: FORMALISM

Though strictly speaking there are Formalists dating back to the time of Kant, Formalism as it is known today may be regarded as a fairly recent view, made famous by the school of criticism known as the *New Critics*. Unlike its predecessors, Formalism takes seriously the problem of artist intention (to one degree or another dependent on the aesthetician, of course). Of the recent Formalists, the most famous is Clive Bell and his theory of "Significant Form." (We met him in the earlier chapter on aesthetic experience.) Less famous, but still quite influential, are the theories of G. E. Moore, and Roger Fry, clear Formalists, and Monroe C. Beardsley, who, while relying quite heavily on the form of an object for establishing it as art, adds in other things.

The shift is interesting: aestheticians and critics are no longer immersed in understanding whether something is art or not *from* the perspective of the artist or the creative process. Instead, the focus is now on the object, the artwork. There are two avenues along which Formalism may travel. One is to discuss the object merely as a construction, focusing on the properties the object has and the relationships of those properties, but only insofar as they are able to be perceived through simple sensory contact with the object. The other avenue, the one more traveled, focuses on how the object affects its audience. Analyses of this sort are called "reception" theories, alluding to how the audience *receives* the artwork or how they experience the artwork. In the case of some Formalists, like Bell, such analyses are called "arousal" theories, given that the artworks arouse in the viewer some state. If the audience is affected in a certain way, based in this case on how and what the object itself actually is, what properties it objectively possesses, then the work is truly art. Furthermore, how the audience is affected is much more accessible to aestheticians and critics than is the intent of the artist. First, there is always an audience about (more or less). Second, the Formalist is interested in how the audience *actually* is affected. One is then not in the position of having to access some private individual artistic intention. The shift instantiated by the Formalists is away from the (possibly inaccessible) artist and the process of creation and *toward* the (accessible and present) audience.

According to the New Critics, what a work represents, what is in the mind of the artist, what the religious or moral climate is, what the history of the presentation of the work is, what others have said about the work—all these items, while interesting and perhaps important in *criticism* of the work, are not necessary in order to determine the status of the object as art. The only elements necessary to determining the status are contained *in the work itself.* These are completely accessible to any viewer of the work (any one with working senses), regardless of her previous knowledge or her religious, moral, metaphysical, or other commitments. The work itself, standing alone, is the key to its constitution as art. This makes the determination of the status all the more certain and a good deal easier. Elements contained in the work are accessible to anyone with functioning senses.

G. E. MOORE

George E. Moore, who worked in England in the first half of the 20th-century England, was one of the first Formalists of this period. Moore begins his aesthetics with the notion that aesthetic contemplation—experiencing and appreciation—is an *intrinsic* good, a good on its own (as distinguished from an *instrumental* good, or a good for something else). Aesthetic consideration is good because it combines two ingredients: emotion, which, for Moore, seems to *essentially* accompany attention to an art object, and cognitive appreciation of beautiful qualities. These beautiful qualities exist in objects themselves, and Moore sets out to explain what they are.

Moore describes a broad criterion for what makes an object beautiful. Objects are beautiful if they possess *organic unity*. Works that have organic unity, or a sort of "wholeness," are works of art. The parts themselves have a certain value, but when they are put all together, the value of the whole is greater than the sum of the parts. Moreover, the degree of the unity is the criterion of evaluation of the work as art. However, for our purposes, the fact that it constitutes the work as art suffices. For an object to be an object of art is for it to

(1) be an artifact, and
(2) be an organic whole, that is, possess organic unity.

The possession by an object of a certain characteristic, such as organic unity, is not unique to Moore. Bell also attributes to objects the status of art on the basis that they contain a certain objective property.

CLIVE BELL

Like Moore, Clive Bell takes seriously the position of the viewer in determining whether a thing is art. This is, in principle, a very sound position from which to determine the status of some object. This is because it is the position in which most all of us find ourselves vis-à-vis art. When we ask "Is this art?" we are, more times than not, asking ourselves the question: "Do I believe this is art?" This is an interesting question when attempting to determine whether some object is worthy of our serious aesthetic consideration, but it is equally interesting when our motive is determining whether we hang it in our gallery, hang it in our church or synagogue, express approval of its being funded by our tax dollars, or establish its monetary value.

Bell's criterion for whether something is art is whether it contains a central ingredient, both necessary *and* sufficient for establishing the work as art. If the object contains *Significant Form*, then the work is art. If it fails to contain the objective property of Significant Form, then it is not art. It is a simple analysis: For an object to be a work of art is for it to

(1) be a work possessing Significant Form.

The words 'Significant Form' are capitalized because of the special nature of the concept. Significant Form is that property of an object that *changes and colors the viewer's experience*. It makes the viewer experience, or feel, *aesthetically*. Only works of art can provoke or prompt viewers to feel this way.

It is not as though the work has some special power. Instead, Bell tells us that what provokes this special aesthetic emotion is just what we can sense: certain lines, shapes, colors, melodies, harmonies, symmetries, and so on. The having of these elements in the correct manner is what it means for the object to possess Significant Form. And viewers will, when viewing objects that possess Significant Form, experience this aesthetic emotion.

By Significant Form, Bell does not mean beauty. He says that beauty is a broader category; things other than art objects—like flowers and sunsets—can be beautiful. Furthermore, beautiful things, Bell suggests, are always attractive. This need not be the case with objects possessing Significant Form. In perceiving the Significant Form of an object, we see the necessity of the connections, the rightness of the object. And only when we experience this can we say that Significant Form is present. The new analysis is for an object to be an art object is for it to

(1) be an artifact, and

(2) be a work possessing Significant Form.

Bell admits that his theory seems subjective: if Sam sees Significant Form in an object and Sally does not, then the object will be art for him but not for her. The solution is to rely on the sensible properties that the object actually possesses as the key for giving rise to the feeling of Significant Form. Since it is the *object* that contains the Significant Form, and since the object does not undergo any substantial physical changes between Sam's and Sally's viewing it, then the presence or absence of the feeling of Significant Form is to be explained through differences *in them* as the viewers, not in the object. If one does not detect Significant Form, then the best explanation would be that one is (1) not paying attention, (2) sensibly nonfunctioning in some way, or (3) conceptually/cognitively nonfunctioning. This frees the view from a gross subjectivism.

However, there exists a problem, seemingly unique to Bell's Formalism, that does not dissolve so easily. It would seem, and Bell has been charged with this by more than one philosopher (for example, Noel Carroll), that the account of Significant Form is fatally *circular:* The presence of Significant Form is detected only when one experiences the "Significant Form Emotion."

But the only way to experience the Significant Form Emotion is to be in attendance to some work with Significant Form. Significant Form, then, does little work to define the Significant Form Emotion, since the Significant Form Emotion is defined in terms of the Significant Form.

If Bell's analysis fails, it at least stands as a benchmark for a tradition called *Aestheticism*. Aestheticism holds that what constitutes an art object is that object's ability to create certain viewer experiences, or "aesthetic experiences." There are, however, some initial problems with Aestheticism as an approach to defining art. The first is the one that appears to plague Bell: attempting to divorce the definition of what is in the work that triggers the experience in us from the experience itself. Another problem is the subjectivity that Aestheticism can foster: Stronger positions of Aestheticism than Bell's might make the same work susceptible to being a work of art to one viewer and not to another. Finally, Aestheticism has been accused of confusing whether an object has some broadly artistic characteristic, like beauty or aesthetic merit or aesthetic power, with whether the object is or is not art. Bell, however, is a weak Aestheticism theorist, and this is also the case with Monroe Beardsley (whom we met in chapter 1, in the discussion of aesthetic experience, and whom we will see again in the Formalism section of chapter 8, in defining "beauty.")

FORMALISM CONSIDERED

Formalism is an important step in the investigation of what makes an object an art object. It is important because it focuses more on the work itself and the reactions of the audience attending to that work. It attempts to ignore as superfluous to determining the status of the object elements such as artist intention and background of the creation or presentation of the object. The focus is, in a strictly Formalist analysis, just on the work itself, and on the properties, *and the relationships among those properties*, of the work.

Formalism developed, with New Criticism, as a means of escaping the metaphysical and intentional commitments that came with the earlier theories of Romanticism and Expressionism. Given Modern artistic trends, representation by this time was virtually dismissed as a theory of art. With the artistic movement of Impressionism came a more feeling-oriented view of what makes something art. Formalism, then, allowed for greater precision in determining whether an object—on its own—was art, and it attempted, at least in the strictest formulations, to retain an objectivism. By "objectivism" here is meant a focus on the properties of the object itself as essential to constituting its status as art. Formalism, though, was not free from difficulty.

Aside from the problems mentioned above, Formalism apparently suffers from two distinct difficulties. First, although it is easy to concentrate on the form of something like a musical composition, it is difficult to view a visual work that is obviously a representation purely as a formal construct. It is difficult to view David's famous portrait of Socrates and see anything other than Socrates (and the rest of his group). It is hard to see lines, shapes, colors, and so forth, when the portrayal of Socrates is so obvious. It is even difficult in many Impressionist and Postimpressionist works to not see, say in the case of Monet, haystacks or Westminster Palace, or even in the case of Turner, not to see, say, angels or ships. And this may be even more difficult when it comes to something like a theatrical play.

Perhaps this could be remedied with a weaker reading of Formalism, wherein we might say that although imitation is perfectly legitimate to attend to either in the pursuit of appreciation or criticism, it is not relevant to the establishment of the object as art. The problem here is that it substantially weakens the thesis past the point where any of the known Formalists went. Furthermore, it is not even clear that the weak thesis can survive. Why, we would ask, ought we to pay attention only to the formal elements in determining the status of some object as art? Why not pay attention to the fact that the work actually does depict, say, Socrates? If no answers are forthcoming, then the Formalist account suffers.

SECTION SIX: ANTIESSENTIALISM

Twentieth-century Antiessentialists contend that there is nothing that all works of art share. This is their *negative* claim: that there is no single essence of art. If all art objects were put in a set, then there is nothing that relates all the members of that set together except that they are each called 'art', 'art-work', or 'art object'. Are all art objects beautiful? No. Are all art objects imitative or representative? No. Are all art objects emotionally expressive? No. Are all art objects human-made? Perhaps, but then so are lawn mowers and food processors. (Some, of course, would argue that not all art objects are human-made; some may be natural.) From their failure to articulate a single feature that all art objects share in common *and* from the challenge of art in the 20th century to consciously and volitionally challenge every conception of what makes a thing art, the Antiessentialist raises the claim that nothing is *the* essence of art.

However, the Antiessentialist does not make *only* the negative claim. She also makes—and must make—some positive claim. This is to avoid becoming the "Nondefinition," that art is whatever one says it is (we took up this discussion in the first section of this chapter). No matter how modest a positive claim it is, Antiessentialism, to purport to be a true answer to the question "what is art?" must offer something positive.

Three possibilities present themselves. (1) There are *many* definitions of art, all equally legitimate, such that if any object falls under any one of the definitions, then it is art (which can be expressed as a series of disjuncts: "Art is x *or* y *or* z"). (2) There is no single feature shared by all art objects, but many art objects share with other art objects certain features, making a *family* out of art. (3) Or art is a concept that is *open* and must *evolve*, so that while there may be, say, disjunctive definitions that we might offer today, these same disjuncts may not hold tomorrow. In this section, we will briefly explore these possibilities and the prescription that Antiessentialism offers for the future of philosophizing about the question, What is Art?

LUDWIG WITTGENSTEIN'S INFLUENCE

Historically, the trend toward Antiessentialism began earlier than the 20th century. Most aestheticians would place it with Ludwig Wittgenstein and his theory of *family resemblances*. Wittgenstein's theory of family resemblance does not specifically address the problem of defining 'art'. His theory was about essences in general, not specifically about the essence of art. However, it is his general philosophical interest in the prospects and possibilities of essentialism in all forms that gave rise to a "family resemblance" kind of Antiessentialism as a theory of art. What Wittgenstein did was to provide a philosophical mechanism—the notion of the family resemblance—that we may apply to the question of art.

Wittgenstein advocates the position that essences do not exist. You will recall that in discussing Plato and Schopenhauer, we referred to the Forms or Ideas. Forms are the real *essences* of, among other things, particular natural objects. Each of the items found in the natural world has an essence. Every chair participates in an essence of what it is to be a chair, or "chair-ness," and so forth. And this is how it is supposed to be with art, too. Every physical instance of art participates, for Plato at least, in the *essence* of "art-ness." Definitions that try to get at a single nature common to all artworks are, in a sense, attempting to articulate the essence of art. Now, not all philosophers of art who are attempting to define 'art' believe in Platonic Forms. Aristotle believed that there was an essence to art, but that it was to be found within all physical or instantiated art objects. Essences can still exist without the metaphysical commitments entailed by, say, a Platonic or Schopenhauerian system. Any analysis that states that there is an articulatable commonality that all artworks exhibit is in the tradition called "essentialism." And this is why the tradition arguing that there is no essence to art is called *Antiessentialism*.

Wittgenstein is a member of this camp. However, he did not believe that patterns, resemblances, general common features, and so forth cannot be found among differing objects all apparently correctly labeled as (say) 'art'. The problem is that when any single one of these patterns or common features is explored as a possible definition of art, counterexamples are always found. A *single* commonality is impossible to find.

But instead of simply denying that there are similarities among artworks, we may introduce the Wittgensteinian theory of *family resemblances*. A family resemblance may be explained in a couple of ways. First and most obviously, consider your own family. Perhaps you have brothers and sisters. While your brothers and sisters all bear some resemblance to you and your parents, they do not all resemble one another in every detail. There are probably several characteristics that you do not share with your siblings. Furthermore, it may be the case that while your brother has features that each of your parents have, and you do too, you have *no* features in common with your brother. We do not think that on this basis you are unrelated to your brother or your other siblings. Instead, we say that there is a family resemblance between you and your siblings, and that some shared characteristics, while not all, ground the relationship you bear to your siblings.

Take another example, one that Wittgenstein himself discusses: the idea of a *game*. Try as we will, says Wittgenstein, it is impossible to give any definition of 'game' for which we will not find some counterexample. Though many games involve competition, not all do. Though many games involve human interaction, not all do. Some are based on chance, some on skill. However, it is not hard to identify adequately and noncontroversially objects as 'games'. ("I know one when I see it.") Perhaps artworks, while all equally correctly labeled 'art', share no single feature, like games, but share a group of features, each instance of art having some of the features common to other artworks, but missing some features that other artworks have.

If art is considered in this manner, then we may see some art objects as falling under one definition of art, while other works might well fall under other definitions. Perhaps there are a large set of definitions under which an object is determined to be art. This is to offer a *disjunctive definition* of 'art'. For an object to be an art object is for that object to

(1) be A or be B or be C or be D, and so forth until the list of possible definitions is exhausted.

There is the possibility that the list will be exhausted, given that there are a finite number of artworks, and there always will be a finite number of artworks. However, the list could potentially become very large, and with its growth the possibility of identifying all the As, Bs, and Cs (etc.) included in such a definition becomes increasingly difficult.

This sort of definition is generally called a disjunctive definition because it is composed of "disjuncts": definitions separated by the connective "or." Any one of these disjuncts, when applicable, is all that an object need possess in order to rightly be called 'art'. If none of the disjuncts applies, then the object is not art. If one or more applies, then the object *is* art.

Of course the trick is to specify the content of each of the various disjuncts. Without that move, the project is incomplete. What Wittgenstein was attempting to do was to offer a *form* for defining objects related on one another, related by word or by concept. But if we are to take seriously a disjunctive definition of art, then the disjuncts will have to be specified. We do not know all the disjuncts. We might speculate that they would include representation, imitation, expression, symbolism, semiology (sign making), and on and on. But we would be hard pressed to think through all the permutations. And, supposing we were to tackle and finish the job, would there be artists ready to challenge our list? Would we would have to continue to add disjuncts to our list in order to account for challenges?

MORRIS WEITZ

A sort of disjunctive definition is offered by Morris Weitz. He suggests this not primarily because of the wealth of counterexamples that can seemingly be leveled at any given definition, but because 'art' itself is a concept that continues to evolve. If we attempt to place boundaries on what constitutes art, we set ourselves up for refutation, because in attempting to install a boundary, we do nothing but construct something artificial and alien to the nature of art. Simply put, in constructing a boundary, we today do little but challenge tomorrow's artists to defeat that boundary. Art changes and grows, so any definition we might assert would need to change and grow as well.

It is the evolutionary aspect of increasing disjuncts that restrains interest in developing and specifying the content of each of the disjuncts. Though one may, with historical study and identification of patterns, be able to construct a disjunctive definition of all art up to the present, art is still being created. If Arthur Danto is wrong, and we are not at the end of art, then presumably more disjuncts will have to be added to the list of current ones. However, if Danto is right, then perhaps there is a possibility of identifying the disjuncts. We need to understand that the question about the nature of art is completed only when we fill in or identify the nature of each disjunct. The form alone will not satisfy our interest in the traditional question, "What is Art?"

Weitz's contention that no essence can be found because art is an open, evolving concept has come under attack. Maurice Mandelbaum suggests that if we take Wittgenstein's notion of family resemblances together with the family analogy, we see that while, say, Sally and her brother share no features, they do have parents in common (and so similar DNA patterns). Mandelbaum suggests that although there may be, in the notion of family resemblances, instances of artworks that bear no similarity to one another, they would, like Sally and her brother, have commonalities *in ancestry*. It would follow that if we can get to the beginning of art, we may be able to find this common ancestry, where all artworks would share some essence, some nature, with their common roots. Now, this suggestion itself has apparent problems. First, it is only a *logically* possible solution, perhaps not a practically possible solution. It may be historically impossible to find this common ancestry. Moreover, proponents of the view that art changes through revolutions might analogize *that* to some "family or genetic mutation," where an offspring might bear no similarity at all to its parentage. No connection could be described, and so the chain would not continue back in the way it must for Mandelbaum's suggestion to work. Art is obviously changing—or has obviously done a great deal of changing—and its categories must change in concert with art itself. And it is this empirical fact that seems to fuel the work of such Antiessentialists as Weitz.

SECTION SEVEN: THE ARTWORLD

The tradition of Antiessentialism may be seen as the motivation behind the theory of art called, all inclusively, the Artworld Theory. Artworld theorists, such as Arthur Danto and George Dickie, argue that Antiessentialism is incorrect, that art is not indefinable. They argue that while there may not be a nature common to all artworks per se—that is, as objects—there is something common to all artworks: their position in the Artworld. Part of what is so interesting in this Artworld tradition is the shift that we are here encountering.

(1) At the beginning, art was simply imitation of nature. This was an *objective* definition; "objective" because it put the onus for the determination of whether something was art on the *object*. If the object was an imitation of nature, then it was art.

(2) Next, we see in Romanticism and Expressionism a shift toward the *subjective*: Objects are art at least partly because they are *intended* by the artist to be art *and/or* produce some effect in the audience.

(3) In Formalism, we see a shift back toward objectivism through the attempt to determine the status of the object merely on the basis on the object itself. While there are obvious cross-overs to the reception of objective properties by the object's audience—as in the case of Bell's Significant Form—the focus is still principally on the object and the properties it possesses.

(4) And now—if we can leapfrog Antiessentialism—the Artworld theorists make another shift, this time back to the subjective: The shift here is not toward the *individual*, however, but toward the collective body of subjects, or the collective body of all viewers, hearers, and so forth.

This constant shifting between the object as determiner of its status, the artist as determiner, and the audience as determiner is interesting because it demonstrates a need to find some lasting and stable, *though accessible*, foundation upon which to build a theory of art. This last shift, the shift toward the collective subject, is the topic for this last section in our attempt to find the answer to the question, What is Art?

ARTHUR DANTO AND THE ARTWORLD

Arthur Danto begins by suggesting that artworks are principally *vehicles for aesthetic interpretations*. This does not mean that every artwork must be interpreted, or a meaning to every artwork must be offered. Instead, for an object to be an artwork it must be *seen* to be an artwork. It must be *interpreted* as an artwork. When Danto considers the world of art around him, he sees the work of such artists as Marcel Duchamp, Robert Rauschenberg, and Andy Warhol. What makes, he asks, the Brillo pad box that Warhol created—

created to imitate exactly the Brillo pad box found in any supermarket—art, while the supermarket box is not art? What makes the show shovel that Duchamp displays under the name *In Advance of a Broken Arm* a work of art, while the show shovels in the hardware store, ones that have all the same perceptual properties as the Duchamp artwork, are not art?

What accounts for the difference between the Warhol box and the supermarket box, Danto suggests, is a *theory of art*. Without a theory of art, without a theory of how to identify art, the Warhol box and the supermarket box would not be different. The Warhol box is *interpreted* as a work of art. The supermarket box is not. It is the interpretation as art that makes the Warhol box art. This goes for Brillo pad boxes as well as for portraits. The interpretation transforms, or as Danto puts it, *transfigures* an object, be it an ordinary object like a Brillo pad box or a portrait, into art. Without interpretation, there is no art. By "interpreting a work of art" Danto is speaking about understanding how that work comes to be regarded as a work of art—or, more precisely, how that work of art *fits into the tradition* of art.

For Danto, the Artworld is not merely a collection of people, places, or things. It is not merely an institution existing today. It is a *tradition*. Art, to be art, must fit into that tradition. And while the tradition of art—the history and institution of art in all its complexity—is made up of people, places, objects, and events, it is more than that. It is the connection between these things as it is borne out through years of art creation, art appreciation, art criticism, and development of certain canons and conceptions of art.

Danto's theory is not a simple "reception" theory in the way that Bell's theory is. The interpreter, for Danto, is not a single subject, but a *collective subject*. The Artworld is, in part, a living, changing institution, a subjective collective, consisting of artists, critics, patrons, audiences, art historians, curators, producers/directors, art guild members, aestheticians, and probably sociologists and anthropologists. But the Artworld is also the interpretative tradition itself, an historical progression, an institution not merely made up of people and objects but also of *time* and *history*. Danto is describing a great community that persists through time and is so diverse that it encompasses everyone from the Sunday viewer to Rembrandt. It is through the presentation and acceptance of an art interpretation of any object by the Artworld that an object is established as art.

Certainly one apparent difficulty with Danto's Artworld analysis of the nature of art and interpretation is the scope with which we are dealing. The Artworld is not a tangible entity, so it is difficult to specify in hard terms the mechanisms involved with an object fitting into the Artworld. It is difficult to specify *when* and *why* a given object becomes art, especially when we are describing recent works. There is little contention regarding the place of the *Mona Lisa* in the Artworld. But there may be a good deal of discussion raised about some object created yesterday in New York's Soho district, today being considered for a space in the Museum of Modern Art. How precisely need we define the mechanisms involved in Danto's Artworld and its transfigurative power?

Another apparent difficulty, mentioned earlier, derives from the fact that the *interpretation* that we continue to discuss is not merely a conference of art-status. This conferrence of art-status is indeed a part of the interpretation process; it may even be presupposed in the offering of any interpretation. But what we generally mean when we use the term 'interpretation' is that we are in some way determining the *meaning* of the object. In the case of *In Advance of a Broken Arm*, for those who consider the object art, the *interpretation* or *meaning* that stands behind the presentation of the object is of primary, and perhaps solitary, importance in determining its status as art. The statement made by *In Advance of a Broken Arm* or the Brillo pad box is what is important.

It might seem that for the interpretation to establish the nature of the object as art, we need to be fairly clear on the correct interpretation. Danto says the best interpretation is the one closest to the one the artist intends. However, in saying this, Danto allows back in the problems that seem to plague intentionalist analyses, theories explicitly referring to what was in the mind of the artist at the time of creation of the artwork. How do we know which interpretation is the correct one, *and* does this determination not play a role in whether the interpretation does indeed confer on the object the status of being art?

In any event, Danto's analysis is an encouraging and engaging one that is motivated to defeat the Antiessentialist and that may well succeed in this. The determining of an object to be art is found in how it is received by this community and tradition, the Artworld. For an object to be an art object is for it to

(1) be interpreted as art by the Artworld.

Just a note before we move on: It is interesting to see the importance of art interpretation in Danto's theory reflect the focus on interpretation found in other contemporary aesthetic interpretive enterprises, such as Deconstructionism. Perhaps similar to the Artworld theorist, the Deconstructionist attempts to understand the role of art through its meaning or interpretation. In both, the interpretation depends not so much on the object itself, but on the tradition in which the interpreting is done. Without the interpretation, there is no art. Moreover, in that a single object can be successfully interpreted in a number of ways, there can be, for a single object, a number of artworks.

Deconstructionists like Jacques Derrida, Paul DeMan, and Stanley Fish suggest that the question "What does this work mean?" is ill constructed. First, we cannot come to understand *the* meaning of the object, since there is no single meaning to be found. There is no referent, standing outside the interpretation, of any given text or object. There can indeed be *many* meanings. And in the presentation of different meanings the conventions of symbolism and the expectations of those doing the interpreting are revealed. With different interpreters—with different backgrounds—different interpretations can be found, and given the diversity in grounding each one, a decision about which of two is the best is not only impossible, it is ludicrous. We do not take the artist, determine her intent, and have the meaning. Nor can we take the object, and in attending to it closely, understand its meaning. Meaning is not objective; meaning is subjective. And with the subjectivity comes a huge wealth of possibilities in terms of interpretation, and all perhaps relative to a single object.

The explanations Derrida and DeMan offer are certainly more complex than these. However, the point that interpretations cannot be fixed or stabilized is made even on simple grounds. Danto is not a Deconstructionist. This is obvious in his assertion that the best interpretation is the one closest to that of the artist himself. However, it is nonetheless interesting to see how Deconstructionism can be seen to parallel the importance Danto places on interpretation.

GEORGE DICKIE AND THE INSTITUTIONAL DEFINITION OF ART

Though there is a difference in trappings, George Dickie's view appears in substance much like Danto's. There are key differences, however. The criticisms that some make against Danto differ from those against Dickie, and vice versa. Danto's Artworld is a tradition, a history of art. Dickie's Art Institution is less historically described. Dickie's is not a tradition or a history, but an institution. And, primarily, it is an institution made up of people, and it is understandable from today's perspective.

The Art Institution is not, says Dickie, an institution as in the sense of a society or corporation. It is, though, an institution in the sense of an *established practice*. It is not the sort of institution of which one can have a fixed understanding; it is constantly changing, constantly evolving, and big. Perhaps, Dickie ventures, the Institution is *all the presenters and all the goers*. However, it is obvious in the attempt to specify the members of this rather large, and perhaps open set, that the best that can be given is still vague. This is a danger in both Danto's and Dickie's conceptions. But Dickie's Institution is still much simpler than the interpretive tradition that is Danto's Artworld.

For Danto, artworks are dependent upon the interpretation(s) they receive through the Artworld. For Dickie, the mere reception into the Artworld itself constitutes the object as art. For an object to be an art object is for it to

(1) be an artifact (explicitly stated),

(2) be a "candidate for appreciation by some person or person acting of behalf of a certain social institution" (the Art Institution).

This is known as his "Institutional Theory of Art." Objects are art objects because of the position they occupy within the Art Institution. One of the chief advantages of an Institutional definition of art is that the relationship that has the power to confer art-status is not merely between the artist and the work, nor it is between the work and the viewer, *nor* is it between the artist, the work, and the viewer, but it is between and among the artist, the work, *all* the viewers, and so many others who have membership in the Art Institution. The Institutional Theory of Art is a broad-based analysis of what makes a thing art.

There are, however, some difficulties with an Institutional analysis. One apparent problem for Dickie's analysis is that if an object is a work of art presented or accepted for aesthetic appreciation, does this mean that all works of art must be appreciated? What about *bad* artworks? Dickie answers this objection: An artwork is not so *because* it is in fact appreciated or judged to have aesthetic merit; an object is a work of art when it is presented and accepted *as a candidate* for appreciation. It is art when it is accepted as an object of aesthetic contemplation. After this acceptance, *then* evaluations are made about how good or bad the work is. So bad works of art can be works of art, given only that they are effectively introduced into the system.

A second apparent problem is the problem of presentation. Since Dickie includes the consideration that the work have conferred on it the status of art *as a work that is a candidate for appreciation*, it may seem that there cannot be anything like an art object that is not presented. There cannot be any objects that are not presented that can be art. Dickie addresses this problem by showing that in the analysis he is not interested in the *actual* presentation of the object, but only in what we might call the *logical* presentation. That is, an artwork is a work that *is of the kind* to be presented. Whether it actually is does not affect its status as art. All it need be is the sort that would, or would normally, be presented to art audiences.

A third apparent problem is raised by Robert Stecker (among others), who questions whether the account offered by Dickie is circular. It would seem that the Artworld is defined in terms of its membership (artists, audiences, critics, et al.). However, these members are defined in terms of their relations with certain objects: artworks. And artworks are defined only in terms of their acceptance by the Artworld. It would seem that there is no clear foundation, some one category or subset of the set 'Art Institution' that can be defined without recourse back to some other part of the Institution. The only item in the analysis that is independently defined is that the object must be an artifact. But of course this does not make any headway into determining art artifacts from nonart artifacts without the second condition that turns on the Art Institution. Dickie knows of this charge of circularity but does not see it as a problem *unless* the concept 'Art Institution' is seriously in question. Since we make ready use of this concept, there does not need to be anything further to our conventional use of the label, replies Dickie. And if we use the term successfully, then it is grounded in the language and need not be defined in an essentialist way in order to function as a condition in the analysis.

A final apparent problem, common to both Artworld accounts, is raised by Ted Cohen. Cohen contends, and understandably so, that the Artworld institution is so vast and so loosely defined that it may be impossible to determine whether this institution has indeed conferred art-status on a thing. While an object that has received such notoriety as *In Advance of a Broken Arm* may be entrenched in the Artworld, what about an object found in Sam's shed that he convinces his curator friend Sally to hang in her gallery? Here a bona fide member of the Artworld, a curator, participates in the presentation of an object, and the object receives attention and comment, and probably *interpretation*, by gallery attenders. Perhaps it even sells; perhaps an art patron buys it and hangs it in her house. Has this object gone through enough stages, touched enough Artworld Institution members, so that it is art? If one's intuition is "yes," then what if it completes only a few of those steps? If one's intuition is "no," then what if Sam's object is reviewed by a major critic? Or makes its way into the National Gallery? Surely then it would be art. The problem is that through the object's journey into and through the Institution of the Artworld, it is hard to pinpoint at what step, if ever, the object truly takes on the status of art.

CHAPTER 5

Creations and Re-creations

In this chapter, we will consider issues that have to do with the creation of works of art as well as the copying and reproducing of works of art. We will begin by talking about one of the most basic issues: creativity.

CREATIVITY

Much can be said about the nature of creativity from a psychological perspective. While our discussion will keep to a philosophical basis, overlap between psychological and philosophical inquiry into creativity is inevitable. In some cases, philosophy acts as a signpost to further empirical study by considering the various possibilities and constructing models of how we might expect the process of creativity to work.

The more common usage of the term "creativity" describes an *attribute* of either the artist or the artwork. One might say that Salvador Dalí was a creative artist, using new images and mixing reality and absurdity to create his surrealism. One might note that his *Hallucinogenic Toreador* is a creative work, that it uses the *Venus di Milo* image, along with the image of a face (look for the mouth and chin in Venus's stomach), in a creative way. What is meant is that the artist has the ability to *create original or novel works* and that the creative artworks themselves show originality and novelty, and usually cleverness and innovation. When describing a work or artist as creative, we ascribe value to the work or a certain virtue to the artist. By describing Dalí as creative, one might mean that (1) he branched out, perhaps creating a new genre that allows for a new range of artworks that may contribute to rewarding aesthetic experiences, or (2) he has taken something established, perhaps cliché, and re-created it in a new and aesthetically valuable way. In either use, Dalí is identified as having done something positive and having contributed to aesthetic value on the whole.

We also use the word "creativity" to describe the process an artist undertakes to create a work of art. It is interesting to note that many philosophers, specifically those who include artist intentions in their accounts of what makes an object art or what makes a thing beautiful, discuss the creative process. At the beginning, the ancient Greeks thought that creativity was a matter of being divinely inspired by a Muse. The Muse would *speak through* the poet or playwright. Aristotle broke this divine tradition, saying that the process of creation is twofold: First, the artist *imitates* nature, and second, the artist *betters* nature, showing the archetypal or the universal in nature.

Nietzsche believed that art, or the best art, was created only when the artist synthesized the energies of the two forces in nature, the Apollonian and the Dionysian. Tolstoy, while not expounding much on the process of creation, does give us a firm account of one part of the process: The artist must be absolutely sincere in the portrayal of the idea or feeling that he is trying to express. Croce had a more robust sense of creation. He thought that through the formation of an *intuition*, the artist fixes the idea that she will express in the artwork. Collingwood had much the same position. The artist's expression, essentially the creative process itself, *is* the artwork. It is in the Expression Tradition that the creative process and the art itself are most closely aligned.

In a Naturalist account of beauty (which we will discuss in chapter 8), we see allusions to the creative process. For George Santayana, to create a beautiful object is to instill into that object the attribute of pleasure, making pleasure a property of the object. For John Dewey, the creative process is seen in the attempt to build in the viewer the experience of unity. Naturalist accounts focus, by and large, on the experience of the viewer in the face of art. The experience itself may be seen as either a continuance or a mirror of the creative process. What we do in viewing art is to reconstruct for ourselves the creative process. We take the object and see in it the inspiration, development and ultimate embodiment of the artwork. If this is what the aesthetic experience truly is, then it is principally a *reliving* of the act of creation over and over again.

The creative process seems to have three elements: the inspiration, the development, and the embodiment. Each phase is essentially a different project. In the first phase, the artist may be passive or active. An idea for an artwork might simply *dawn on her.* Perhaps she sees something extraordinary in nature, or perhaps she sees something ordinary in a new light, and she is inspired to create an artwork. On the other hand, an artist searching for an idea may take definite and systemic steps toward building an idea for artistic embodiment. If Sally has a deadline for producing a commissioned work, she may not be in the position of waiting until something dawns on her. Sally may have to build her own inspiration.

The second phase is development. The *idea* must be developed. What does the artist want to show, communicate, mean, tell? Perhaps she wants to incorporate a lesson or a message, or perhaps she only wants to make people feel a certain way when they look at her work. After these decisions, the artist must develop her ideas with regard to their embodiment. What medium should be used? What musical instruments? What colors? What musical keys? What size? What brushes? What length? What musical or poetic imagery? The artist has many decisions to make in this second stage, perhaps the most cerebral and intensive part of the creative process.

The third phase is embodiment, or, with "nonautographic" arts (we will discuss these directly below), preparation of the instruments that will lead to physical embodiment. Some artists complete the artwork, as an ideal, in the second (developmental) stage, and the only task left is getting it into some physical medium. But these cases seem exceptions to the rule. More often the case may prove to be one in which the artist continues to make development decisions throughout the period of embodiment. Changes are almost inevitable in any artistic plan, and usually those changes increase the aesthetic value of the work. As the artist paints, composes, sculpts, or writes, she is aware of the work in a more concrete way than ever before, and she is able to effect changes that make the work better.

FAKES AND FORGERIES

There is a difference between a fake and a forgery. Different writers attempt to construct this differently, but for this discussion, a fake is a copy of a single work of art intended by the copier to pass for that original artwork. A forgery is a work meant by the forger to pass for a work of another artist. Forgeries need not be fakes: for years, works of Han Van Meegeren were taken to be authentic works of Jan Vermeer. Van Meegeren's works were not copies of actual Vermeer works; Van Meegeren's works were simply very closely in the Vermeer style.

When discussing fakes, we commonly think of single copies being made of single works. If an artwork can only exist in one embodiment, it is called an "autographic" work. An autographic work is a work of which there can be only one: there can only be one *Mona Lisa*, one *Pietà*. This is contrasted with objects like novels, musical compositions, theatrical plays, and visual prints. For instance, there are many copies of *The Adventures of Huckleberry Finn*, many performances of Beethoven's *Ninth Symphony*. When talking about fakes, we are discussing only *autographic* artworks.

The common view on the practice of creating fakes and forgeries is that it is wrong and deceptive and that its products are of low value. If a curator finds that an object in her museum is a forgery, she may be inclined to remove and destroy it. If someone finds that she owns a forgery, she may be very unhappy indeed. When additions are made to museums or to our own collections, we mean to be adding the real things, the authentic works created by the artists we take them to be created by. There is only one true art object (in the case, say, of a painting), and it was created *by the hand of the artist*, and no other object, no matter how perceptually indistinguishable, can be accepted as a substitute.

Why? Suppose that the forgery is a nearly exact copy of the authentic work. And suppose that one bought the forgery (thinking that it was an original) because of the aesthetic value of the work, because she aesthetically appreciated the object. Now, if the forgery is so close and one appreciates the object aesthetically, why should she be bothered by whether it is an original or not? If it still provides her with the same aesthetic experience, whether original or forgery, then is there really a difference? Of course there is a difference. But the difference does not seem to be one borne on just the perceptual differences between original and forgery. If the forgery is any good, the perceptual differences will be negligible. The difference has something to do with the *history* of the object itself.

So why is the *Mona Lisa* worth such an enormous amount—if it is not priceless—while a copy or forgery, even a good one, is worth little? If there is no difference in the perceptual properties of the original and a good copy, then why is one in the Louvre and the other not fit to hang in the most modest museum?

One avenue by which to answer this question is to distinguish between the art object as a *physical object* and as a *sensible or perceptual object*. While there can be only one physical object that is *the Mona Lisa*, there may be many objects that perceptually resemble it. While one might have the same aesthetic experience in viewing the actual *Mona Lisa* as in viewing a good copy—seeing similar properties, for example, or knowing that it was painted during the Italian Renaissance by Leonardo da Vinci—the experience is attached not to the one physical object that is the *Mona Lisa*; the experience is attached to the perceptual object, the object one is (just) looking at. The copy has similar sensible properties to the original, and it shares in the same history because in looking at the copy one may think of the Renaissance and Leonardo. So the experience of seeing the *Mona Lisa* in the Louvre and seeing the copy in a bookshop might be similar. *This is treating the* Mona Lisa *as a perceptual object.*

If the *Mona Lisa* is treated as a *physical object*, then it is recognized that there is only one *Mona Lisa*, only one object actually painted by Leonardo, actually painted during the Renaissance, and actually hanging in the Louvre. The *financial* worth attaches onto the physical object. The *aesthetic* value attaches onto the perceptual object. So while the *Mona Lisa* might be worth a tremendous amount, it could be equal in *aesthetic value* to any of a number of particularly good copies. This distinction between the artwork as a *physical object* and as an *aesthetic object* explains why originals are more valuable than copies, why they are revered and protected, and why copies are not so protected. It is not that the originals are necessarily *aesthetically* more valuable, but because of their unique histories, they occupy special places in the Artworld.

Another important distinction between originals and copies (or forgeries) is found in the way each is judged *relative to the other.* The aesthetic evaluation of an artwork may take into account the basic perceptual properties of that object, its formal relations, and so forth. It might extend to include consideration of the object's historic relations, relations to others of its genre, interpretations of the object, and perhaps the artist's intentions. However, in the evaluation of a copy or forgery, the first criterion of judgment is "How well does it resemble the original?" This has been alluded to all along by talking about *good* copies. This is because the copy is first and foremost an object in relation to the original. Without the original, it stands to reason, there is no copy. And the copy is judged, from the beginning, against the original. The original may bear a relation to the copy, but only insofar as copies happen to be made. The copy is ultimately dependent on the original, *but the original, or the status of the original, does not change at all in spite of the fact that it is copied.* The *Mona Lisa* would be the *Mona Lisa* were there no copies or a million.

One final avenue for addressing the difference between the original and the copy or forgery is found in the artist. The artist who created the original created something unique, an item that added something new, and perhaps quite valuable, to the world. The copier does not do this. She merely adds one-more-of-the-same to the world. If the artist's intention or expression is important in giving the object the status of *art object*, then this could be a basis for determining why the original has a different status than the copy. The copy does not have the same *creative history*, the same contemplation and *molding* that the original has. The artist is one who produces something wonderful: art. The copier produces something whose value is parasitic on the value of the original. While the artist may need various extraordinary qualities—technical skill, insight, and a feel for her materials and what she wants to produce—the copier or forger needs only the technical skill called for in making an object that closely resembles its original.

If the origins of an object make a difference to the status of that object, as the Expression theorist would maintain, then there is a strong basis for saying that the original is superior to the copy, no matter how much the copy resembles the original—or even if the copy *improves* on the original. While a symphony might be improved by the variations of a particularly skillful conductor, by the introduction of new instruments, or by a new arrangement, the creative credit for the work must go to the original artist. It is her expression, and she deserves the credit.

On the other hand, if an object is changed significantly, then that object ceases to be a copy and takes on its own status as an artwork—an *original* artwork—and the relationship it bears the original that inspired it is not "original-to-copy" but "inspiration-to-new-artwork." Stanley Kubrick's film *2001: A Space Odyssey* is not the same artwork as Arthur C. Clarke's novel. Kubrick adapts the novel in such a way as to create a new artwork. But this inspiration relationship need not move from one artistic medium to another. Mozart composed variations on works by other composers. However, the credit for those variations is given to Mozart, not because he is more famous, but because he changed the work substantially enough to make a whole new artwork.

The boundary between simple variation/imprecise copying and this inspiration-relation is founded on the amount of artistic creativity that the second artist infuses into the work of the first artist. The inspired artist creates something new because she *creates*. The mere copier, who does not create, must not be given the aesthetic credit that the inspired artist receives.

A final comment needs to be made regarding the moral difference in tone between "copy" and "fake." There is certainly a difference in the real world between a copy and a fake. A copy is usually made with the original artist's permission, or the permission of the museum or estate to which the original belongs. A copy is usually made with the intention that it be recognized or identified as a copy. A fake, on the other hand, is made without permission and is usually meant *not* to be recognized as a copy, but to *pass* for the real thing. It is meant not to derive its value from the original, as copies do, but to function *as* the original. It is meant to have all the value—aesthetic and monetary—that the original possesses. Now while the monetary worth of copies and undetected fakes are usually quite dissimilar, the *aesthetic* difference between good copies and good fakes amounts to much less. The difference between a copy and a fake is legal and moral, not aesthetic.

REPRODUCTION

Reproduction is quite different from *copying* (whether faking, forging, or something less sinister). When a *copy* is made of an artwork, it is a copy of a work that is *autographic*, and the copy is nothing more than a means of embodying a resemblance of that first original work. When a *reproduction* is made of an artwork, it is of a work that is nonautographic, and in a very real sense is rendering in a perceptual or physical way that nonautographic work. (Unfortunately, the word 'copy' is used widely as a synonym for 'reproduction' especially with regard to verbal works of art, such as in 'copies' of this book.)

An artwork does not exist if it has no perceptual embodiment. If there is no way for us to sense or experience an artwork, then there is no artwork. However, since nonautographic artworks are not identical with musical scores or printing plates—scores are not music and plates are not prints; they are merely the vehicles through which the artworks ultimately exist—we must say that there *is no* artwork when the art is nonautographic and is not *reproduced*. The reproductions *are* the artwork(s).

Some exemplars are better communicated than others. In the case of musical compositions, the exemplar behind the nonautographic artwork is the score, and one can determine the intimacy or distance of the relationship between the exemplar and the reproduction by appealing to the score. One can do the same thing in terms of dramatic productions. And one can appeal to original drafts when determining the reproduction relationship with regard to literature or poetry. These instruments—scores, drafts, plates, and so forth—are not the artworks themselves, but they allow us to identify in a serious way the exemplar, the ideal, of the artwork.

This works in many cases, but not in all. For instance, in dance there exists means for the choreographer to record, like in a musical score, the movements she envisions. One such system is Laban. Unfortunately, this system, or any one of the various dance-recording notational systems, is not widely used. Moreover, until the widespread use of videotaping, the only seriously used medium for transmitting or teaching dance choreography were *actual dancers*, by those who had seen the original choreography *showing* those who wished to learn it, and then having it passed down from teacher to student in that way. (Even with the widespread use of video records, the norm is still person-to-person instruction.) Of course, people forget. And so when it comes to teaching dances they learned to their students, variations on the original choreography are certain to occur. Furthermore, variations are incorporated for a host of pragmatic reasons—the stage is small, the dancer is shorter than the original, the stage is slippery, and so forth. So a dance attributed to Isadora Duncan, passed from student-turned-teacher to student, might end up looking noticeably different from the original Duncan dance. Another difficulty is that the set of dances known as *Swan Lake* might be choreographed by dozens of artists, each one coming up with distinct and perhaps very different productions of the work. However, they are all called *Swan Lake* and apparently correctly so. In cases such as dance, the Artworld seems to accept much greater variety in reproductions. Perhaps this is because of the practical reason that a strict communication of original intent is not possible, not convenient, or that the nature of dance is essentially evolutionary.

Those who advocate this last approach—that an exemplar functions as a point of stability in reproducing nonautographic works—generally believe that certain features must appear for that reproduction to be truly a reproduction. In other words, nonautographic works have *essential* features that must be included in every true reproduction. This allows for the stability. If we are willing to go out on a limb and say that one essential feature of any production of *Swan Lake* is that it is based on the music by Tchaikovsky, then we have identified one essential feature of all reproductions of *Swan Lake*. (One should note that there have been performances called *Swan Lake* that did not use Tchaikovsky's music.) Of course, as we have seen, it is easier to determine the essential features of reproductions if one has scores, drafts, and plates. It is much more difficult to determine, first, if there is no instrument leading to an understanding of the original intent, and second, if variation on the original intent is widely accepted by the Artworld. This is the case with dance.

As there is good and bad copying of autographic art, there is also good and bad *reproduction* of nonautographic art. If a reproduction includes all of the essential features found in the original intent, and all further variations either are in keeping with the tone of the original intent or lead to a higher aesthetic value, then that reproduction is deemed a good one (as a reproduction). If the essential features are not included—or if their exclusion does not contribute in a substantial way to the aesthetic value of the work—and the variations do not increase the value, then that reproduction is a bad one. As in autographic copies, resemblance to the original is a strong point of criticism of a reproduction. However, in nonautographic arts, it is not so easy to determine just what the original is.

PART III

Meaning

Interpreting Art

Mark Rothko, a 20th-century American artist, is best known for his works that feature large areas of single colors on a canvas. His most popular works feature fields of two or three colors. Jackson Pollock, another 20th-century American artist, is best known for his "drip" paintings, made by dripping and splattering paint on a canvas spread out on the floor. Piet Mondrian, a Dutch artist from the 19th and 20th centuries, is best known for his maplike paintings where blocks of vivid color, usually primary colors, are separated by strong, straight black lines. What do these objects mean? What are they about?

In this chapter we will explore facets not found in the immediate sensory experience of the aesthetic object. We will begin exploring the role of the *educated viewer*. The educated viewer may be the professional art critic, the art historian, or simply that person who tries to experience the aesthetic object in some way that transcends an ordinary sensory way. The educated viewer need not have any ability other than the desire to understand the aesthetic object from some other perspective than just looking at it or hearing it. You, as a reader of aesthetics, are an educated viewer.

There is a question about whether it is better to be an educated viewer rather than a "simple, uncontaminated" viewer, one whose knowledge of the object under consideration is limited to her immediate sensory acquaintance-ship with the object. It may seem obvious that it is better to spend time carefully considering an aesthetic object, trying to understand it in more ways than merely visually or auditorially. However, some believe that to attempt to categorize, analyze, or scrutinize a work of art might *lessen* the enjoyment or richness of aesthetic experience that might be felt in a simple sensory appreciation of the object. Some believe that we ought to let art stand on its own.

Say that Sally hears that a great film is coming out. She pays attention to its release date and plans to see it then. She reads the reviews and the press releases. The film is really hyped, making her anticipation all the greater. She expects great things from this film. But when opening day finally comes and she sees the film, she is disappointed. The film, while good, did not live up to the hype. Sally feels cheated. Had she just avoided the hype, she might well have enjoyed a good film. Instead, she cannot get over her disappointment. I am confident that more than a few film students have experienced this when, after hearing again and again that *Citizen Kane* is the best film ever made, they see a film that generally takes more than one viewing and more than casual attention to fully appreciate.

The position that we should approach art objects "uncontaminated" is not too distant from the position of the strict Formalist or the New Critic, who suggests that the object's status as art, and its possession of aesthetic properties, depends solely on what one can appreciate of the object simply by viewing (hearing, etc.) it. Will the educated viewer, on average, have a better experience than the so-called uncontaminated viewer? While our discussion will not attempt to answer this question conclusively—to do so would be to tell audiences what their experiences *should* be, and this is philosophically specious—we will nonetheless examine what it is to be an educated viewer, along with how the education may affect her aesthetic experience. We will discuss what it is to look for something in an artwork or aesthetic object that cannot be found through a simple sensory experience, and what it is to look for connections and relations, to look for comparisons and contrasts in objects.

Art, especially that of the 20th century, has taken a turn for the more cognitive, the more conceptual. Nowadays, art is less about what it looks like and more about what it *means*. When Sam sees Andy Warhol's Campbell's Soup Cans or Warhol's Brillo Pad Boxes, he must ask himself why such mundane objects are elevated to such lofty positions as works of art. (It is common to think of art objects as valuable by virtue of their status as art.) Certainly, the original creators of the soup and box labels were not great and innovative artists. They meant to sell a product. So why is Warhol considered an important 20th-century artist, in large part for his work as a "pop artist"? It would seem that the answer has more to do with the *meaning* that is attached to the display of the soup cans and the boxes, and less to do with what these objects *look* like.

Meanings of artworks are important, and at no other time in the history of art have they ever been more important than in the 20th, and now 21st, centuries. But the question is, What did Warhol *mean* with his soup cans and Brillo boxes? Was he making a social comment on the focal position of the modern kitchen? Was he commenting on the goodness of Campbell's soup and the cleaning efficiency of the Brillo pads? Probably not. The meaning more likely has to do with the mundane character of these objects, something to do with how the line between ordinary objects and art objects is becoming more blurry—something about how the ordinary world and the art world are coming together.

But what about the other *interpretations* offered—the ones about the modern kitchen and the goodness of the products Warhol portrays? What makes these interpretations incorrect? And, furthermore, is it that an artwork can have but a single meaning?

In this section, the terms 'meaning' and 'interpretation' will be used interchangeably. To do otherwise might be to beg the question against a particular position. For instance, if we believe that works of art have meanings, we might be inclined to believe that each work has a singular meaning, and that all interpretations that various educated viewers make that do not reflect that one meaning are incorrect. This is to beg the question against those, like the Deconstructionist, who believe that more than one interpretation may be equally valid.

The views that various thinkers have about meanings and interpretations are broad. At one end of the spectrum are the people who say that to attempt to expound the meaning of a work of art or some other aesthetic object is to harm the experience we might have of that work. They believe that to make the object anything more than what is immediately experienced in simply looking at it is to risk injury to the pleasure that one might experience through attention to that object. Art must stand on its own, and trying to make it more than it is is to do it a disservice. The extremity of this camp needs to be made clear: its members hold that there ought to be no interpretation of the object, no search and no offering of a meaning of the object.

Just next to this camp on the spectrum is the less radical group that *does* allow for meanings of object. However, this group says, every art object has exactly one meaning. That one meaning is fixed by what the artist (composer, author, or other artist) had in mind when she created the object. This is easy to understand. If artworks are essentially expressions of artists' ideas or emotions, then it stands to reason that the meaning of the work is the idea or expression that stands behind it. (Note that it follows that only artifactual artworks have meanings; one needs an artist and her intention in order for the art object to have a meaning.)

Say Sally finds a painting composed of one large black triangle inside a gray circle on a field of white. She might explain that this painting is meant to depict in symbolic fashion the sterility or deadness of those social institutions we consider most stable. And the gray circle represents the corruption spread by these institutions. She might say that the institutions being criticized are the government, the universities, and the educational system. This all makes sense to her, and she offers all of this as the *meaning* of this work. However, suppose that the artist came over and said that Sally completely missed the point. The artist says that the black triangle represents the juxtaposition of stability and uncertainty of new beginning, and the lightening of the surrounding circle and white field are meant to show that as growth occurs, stability is sacrificed and understanding or enlightenment is gained. Chances are that we would take the true meaning of the work to be the explanation given by the artist herself. This is what the "artist's meaning" camp capitalizes on. If artworks are expressions of artists, then who is better to judge the meaning than the artist herself?

The problem is that Sally's explanation, though differing from the artist's, continues to make sense. One may say that while the artist sees one thing—or, more precisely, intends to express one thing—Sally finds that her interpretation is still valuable. It may be valuable because

(A) it shows what *Sally* would have expressed in painting this picture,

(B) it provides for a richer or deeper aesthetic experience in *Sally's* viewing the work,

(C) it makes the painting more aesthetically valuable, by showing a stronger meaning, thereby making more rewarding the experiences of those who follow Sally's interpretation, or

(D) it shows a side of the work that *might* actually have been a part of the expression of the artist *but without her knowledge.*

Though Option (D) is the least obvious, it is still a possibility. Many Expression theorists believe that the artist's work may be the *only possible expression* of her idea or feeling. Now, ideas and feelings can be put into words, but they must first be understood. Perhaps, one might speculate, the artist's expression is beyond words, and perhaps even beyond her own conscious understanding. If the work is the single expression of the artist's idea or feeling, it may be the case that there are items—meaningful items—that are in the work that the artist herself cannot articulate. Since Freud and perhaps before, the idea that there is more to one's mind than can be gained through immediate introspection has been popular. Perhaps the artist, while consciously expressing one thing in her work, *subconsciously* expresses another. If that could be the case, then perhaps the best person to give us the single meaning of the work—the true account of the artist's expression—is not the critic but the artist's psychotherapist!

Appealing to the artist's therapist, if she has one, in order to understand the meaning of a work has never been practiced in art interpretation. (It would violate patient confidentiality anyway.) However, this appeal to a Freudian-Therapist exploration of the artist's *true* intentions, along with the consideration that the artist's intentions might be inaccessible for a variety of other reasons—she is away on holiday, she is dead, she has gone mad—are offered as reasons for *not* putting the sole burden on the artist herself for determining the meaning of a work. This, coupled with the fact that the viewer's interpretation still seems valid even though it differs from the artist's, may lead one to mistrust the camp that says that the artist's intention alone fixes the meaning of her work.

THE INTENTIONAL FALLACY

A strong tradition, supported by the work of William Wimsatt and Monroe Beardsley (1946), states that it is entirely unnecessary to know what was in the mind of the artist when she was creating the work in order to correctly interpret that work. We ought not appeal to the *intentions* of the artist in order to explain the meaning of the work. Instead we ought to consult the objective features of the work. Through an examination of the properties of the object, its formal relations, we will come to a clear understanding of what the object means. So the meaning of Faulkner's *The Sound and the Fury* is what is found in the text itself. The words, and the rules that govern language, give rise to the meaning. The intention of the artist is unnecessary for fixing the meaning of the work. This is the view expressed as the *Intentional Fallacy.*

The question of how much the artist's intentions enter into the validation of any one interpretation is much like the question, "How much does the artist's intention count in terms of establishing some object as a work of art?" Much of the argument against the use of artist intentions in establishing what is art can be mustered against appealing to artist intentions with regard to meaning. Particularly damaging to the use of artist intentions is the general inaccessibility to the artist's intention, because the artist has moved away or died, because the artist's expression encompasses more than she consciously thought, or because of some other reason.

However, some theorists, such as Kendall Walton, believe that Beardsley and Wimsatt, and the formalists they represent, go too far. While Walton and others might agree that the artist's intentions are not the *only* source of developing good interpretations, they suggest that it is at least one avenue. And, indeed, most of us would tend to listen to the artist describe the meaning of her work well before we would listen to someone else.

Antiformalists believe that many other factors might legitimately go into the creation of interpretations. They believe, for a start, that certain facts about the origin of the work contribute to more robust interpretations. Suppose that Sam sees a certain painting that is of lovely Spanish Gothic buildings, streets lined with flowers, and women carrying baskets and bread. He might like this painting, and he might interpret it as a celebration of a certain time and place, or perhaps a celebration of life, or perhaps an expression of the artist's happiness. Suppose though that he were to discover that the artist painted this picture while she was a political prisoner in Cuba. Knowing that fact would probably change the interpretation, or at least give whatever interpretation he offers a greater profundity. Perhaps he might continue to say that the painting celebrated a certain time and place, but he would realize the significance of this celebration in the face of the artist's isolation from this setting, a setting for which she probably had a particular fondness.

Not only may factors such as *origins* and historical relations matter, but also important might be the relations that the work bears to others of its kind. If

Sally hears a work of music that uses the tonal styles associated with Bach and Vivaldi, she may believe that the work is Baroque. In part, she may *evaluate* the work against how good a piece of Baroque music it is. She might also determine the meaning of the work partly on the basis of its time. For instance, she might say that a certain liveliness is characteristic of Baroque compositions, and the presence of this feature shows the mind-set of the Baroque composers. However, suppose that she discovers that the piece was composed just a few years ago. Her interpretation of the work would change. She would look for some reason why such a work would be composed now, for most compositions of the late 20th century do not sound much like classic Baroque music. So it seems that the relations that a work of art bears to others of its kind, or others contemporary with it, may contribute to a richer account of what a work means.

Some who disagree with Beardsley and Wimsatt believe that intentions need not be had firsthand from the artist herself in order to be considered the artist's intentions. Some believe that we often are able to determine the artist's intention without the artist even being alive. When Sam sees Picasso's *Guernica*, he knows without much consideration that the painting depicts tragedy and anguish. And with a bit more attention to detail, he might develop the belief that the tragedy and anguish are the effects of war. It is a safe bet to believe that, regardless of the details, Picasso's intentions were to show the horror of war. One can speculate, and in a fair number of cases, can be correct in speculations as to the artist's intentions.

The problem with such speculation is that it seems to rely solely on the *properties of the work* for determining the artist's intention. If one is simply relying on the object's properties, then why not skip the intermediate step and say that the interpretation is based on the work's features? This is simpler than saying that the interpretation comes from the work's features *as they show the viewer* the artist's intention, from which one then gets her interpretation. Why not simply say that the work's features, through direct consideration of them, give rise to the interpretation?

A PLURALIST CONCEPTION OF INTERPRETATION

To get back to the main point, if we believe that some other explanation of the meaning of a work besides the artist's is legitimate, we move the rest of the way along the spectrum to a more *plural* camp—plural because the position holds that more than a single interpretation or meaning might be equally valid. However, we must be careful to spell out exactly what we mean by a bona fide or legitimate interpretation. At this plural end of the spectrum, we may encounter various arguments for what makes for a correct or bona fide interpretation.

(1) Some believe that *any* interpretation is valid. This, of course, is the most plural camp.

(2) Some believe that any interpretation that is offered by a camp or school of criticism is valid. This is slightly less plural.

(3) Some believe that any interpretation that actually raises the aesthetic experience of at least one person (namely, the one who offers that interpretation) is valid.

(4) Some believe that any interpretation that generally raises the aesthetic experiences of viewers—when they know about it, of course—is valid. Along with this camp is the camp that says "if the interpretation seeks to maximize the aesthetic value of the work," then it is bona fide. Of the plural camps, this is the most conservative.

Option (1) may suffer because it does not appear to serve any real purpose. If Sally interprets the *Pietà* as a commentary on the state of the postal system, she may have something initially interesting, but she has little more. It does not serve any purpose, other than possibly a fanciful one, to incorporate this level of freedom in the interpretation of artworks. What's the point?

Option (2) is a serious option. For the Deconstructionist, the importance of interpretation cannot be minimized. The Deconstructionist believes that the artwork *is* its interpretation. The critic and artist (or *educated viewers* and artist) have a symbiotic relationship. The artwork per se is a product of both of their efforts: the artist creates some embodied point of focus, and the educated viewer attempts to understand and fully experience the work. The Deconstructionist does not believe that there is a single meaning to any work; indeed, the number of meanings are potentially infinite. Even if we were able to consult the artist herself, we would still be in the position of recognizing that the artist's stated intention does not capture the full story. The Deconstructionist denies that there is even a "full story" to be captured. All sorts of considerations might go into determining what would be the *one* meaning, *were this even possible.* But this is not possible. The variables are too broad and far-reaching. So there is no one meaning, but many. And so many interpretations are valid.

This, then, brings us to Options (3) and (4). Option (3) places the focus on the experience and states that the only legitimate interpretations are ones that *create better aesthetic experiences* for the viewer, even on an individual scale. If one's own private interpretation makes her experience of the object at hand more rewarding, then there is a reason to call it legitimate. If aesthetic value is centered in the experience of viewers, as many aestheticians contend, then we need a value-connected reason to include any given interpretation as valid. If one's interpretation makes the experience better, then her interpretation is legitimated.

One apparent difficulty here is that we are returning to allowing just about any interpretation, so long as it raises the experience of any one viewer. This sounds a bit like Option (1). Perhaps Sally's interpreting the *Pietà* as a commentary on the state of the postal system provides a wonderful experience for her because she sees the anguish of the Madonna and she always feels anguish in waiting for her mail, *and* she appreciates that Michelangelo knew that same postal anguish, too. After all, part of what we appreciate in artworks is a sense of connection or the ability of the artist to relate to viewers. *If* we accept such things as contributing to the aesthetic experience, then we might have a reason for adopting a postal interpretation of the *Pietà*. Any interpretation, then, so long as we have a sincere viewer whose experience is heightened by that interpretation, is valid. This makes for an incredibly large number of valid interpretations.

If we are uncomfortable with the extreme plurality of Option (3), we might instead consider Option (4). If a plurality of viewers are involved, rather than just a single individual, we stand a greater chance of having a set of interpretations that are not only finite, but also are manageable. That is, they are manageable because we would be more or less in the position of taking any one of the set of valid interpretations and understanding it. Any one of the set might well raise appreciation of the work, perhaps through making us see the work in a different light.

There is a clear advantage in appealing to a collective base, because the possibility of finding interpretations that have a more solid foundation is more likely. In the postal interpretation, Sally might be the only one to make that connection *ever.* However, in interpreting Burgess's *A Clockwork Orange* as a consideration of moral freedom, one may have a more solid foundation. One can appeal to actual passages in the book to establish a basis for this interpretation. We are not merely adding numbers to Option (3) in moving to Option (4). Instead, we are using the fact that those interpretations that are *most generally* experience-enhancing will find a basis in something that is common to all viewers: specifically, the text, painting, or composition itself.

Basing interpretations on the art object itself may still admit of a plurality of interpretations. The length of the range of interpretations may be illustrated through the case of differing Christian fundamentalists. The Christian fundamentalist believes that the Bible is the absolute and infallible word of God. So how is it, it may be asked, that there are *various* Christian fundamentalist groups, some which differ with others a great deal? This is because a certain amount of Biblical interpretation is inevitable. While each group means to come as close to the actual intent of God as expressed in the Bible as possible, and each pays a great deal of attention to the detail of the text, perhaps going back to the original languages, differences in interpretation are bound to occur. So the moral of this story is that no matter how serious we are in using the text itself to back up the interpretation, other interpretations may still exist, others that pay as much attention to the text as ours do.

In any event, it is with Option (4) that we may find not only the least subjectivist camp, but also a camp that accounts for the value of the viewers' experiences. Option (4)

(A) uses a collective base, not an individual one,

(B) focuses on the properties of the object itself, and

(C) in many formulations, accounts for what we take to be valuable in offering interpretation in the first place: a heightening of the aesthetic experience.

This fourth camp is the view most easily seen as that of the critic.

CHAPTER 7

Censoring Art

Rudy Giuliani, the former mayor of New York, went public with a vocal attack on an art show called *Sensation*, which featured the work of "Young British Artists"—Damien Hirst chief among them—that was on exhibit in the Brooklyn Museum of Art. While Hirst is known for creating highly arresting and sometimes personally revolting works of art (such as displaying animals sliced in half), the mayor's primary focus was on a visual work by an artist named Chris Ofili. Ofili's work is titled *The Holy Virgin Mary*. The depiction of Mary is surrounded by very small pictures of genitalia, and her breast is three-dimensionally constructed of elephant dung. Giuliani threatened to cut off the Gallery's seven million dollar support from the city and have the museum evicted from its space. He called Ofili's work "sick" and "blasphemous." Although he said that his threat was not censorship but rather a correct use of public funds, almost everyone following the story understood this to be a clear case of censorship.

Aesthetic and/or artistic values are not the only considerations that go into assessing the overall value of an artwork. (There is the further question about whether they *ought* to be the only criteria we use in judging art.) Some other value-oriented considerations that commonly come into play when we are having aesthetic experiences or judging works of art include:

- Gender issues
- Ethnic and racial issues
- Religious or spiritual issues
- Social, national, or cultural issues
- Class and power issues

- Political and economical issues
- Moral and ethical issues
- Sexual content
- Violence portrayal

While these sorts of considerations may not enter into formal aesthetic analyses of aesthetic and art objects, they clearly and frequently enter into our experiences of these objects. It is usually because of one (or more) of these sorts of considerations that censorship concerns are raised.

Plato believed that if art has value, its value lies in support of the state. For it to be valuable at all, art must celebrate the virtues of the heroes and the gods. It must demonstrate strength and bravery, and it must never show undue emotion or weakness. If it fails to support the state, it presents only copies of copies, not truth, and it may actually hurt the morale of the citizenry. So, thought Plato, it ought to be censored. Art that does not support the state should not be permitted.

Tolstoy focused on art not in terms of its support of the state as a political unit, but in terms of its support of the society as a moral and religious unit. The artist must, Tolstoy thought, impart to her audience a true sense of the religious attitudes of her society. She must create works that do not conflict with the moral and religious tone of the community. Indeed, she must create works that support this tone. Tolstoy's requirement of art is not dissimilar from the requirement that many conservative thinkers today in America would impose on art. Art, some say, should reflect the real and vital values of the society as a whole. It should not merely reflect the artist's individual values and vision. The artist is only one person. The viewers, however, are numerous. If we live in a democracy, the art of those who portray the sentiments and beliefs of the majority should win out, and that should be the art that flourishes. This flourishing is what is at issue. Much of today's debate regarding art centers upon the use of tax dollars in promoting certain artists and artforms. And one of the most interesting questions of censorship comes out of this debate: Does the government practice de facto censorship when it funds one artist, artform, or art movement, and not another?

Censorship has had a real presence throughout the history of art and societies. Some censorship (enacted by law or otherwise) is apparently justified and necessary. Child pornography and "snuff films" (films of actual murders) are two examples. These kinds of things we find not only morally objectionable, but also extremely reprehensible. The question, though, is: What range should censorship appropriately have? How far are we willing to allow censorship to go? How much of a rein are we willing to put on censorship? The problem is not clear-cut. Many would say that in the United States our expectations are far too strict about what is proper for the artist to produce. Many would say that the guidelines of artistic decency are far too loose. Where is the happy mean, and how can we find it?

OBSCENE ART

Currently the most heated argument centers on the funding and public presentation of works of art that are labeled by some as "obscene." Consider the case of Roger Mapplethorpe, a photographer known for his explicit sexual themes. Much of Mapplethorpe's work seems aesthetically excellent: Some photographs show great composition, balance, lighting, and so forth. The question, though, is whether it is obscene.

Perhaps a more basic question is: Is there such a thing as 'obscene art'? Some observers advocate the view that there is simply no such thing as obscene art. They claim that Mapplethorpe's works are not art *because* they are obscene. This is indicative of the fact that they believe that no obscene object can be art. They believe that such so-called art objects are merely vehicles of obscenity, equal in value to pornography, that is, materials specifically designed to appeal strictly to prurient interests.

Although the works do elicit judgments of obscenity, at least from this group of spectators, this does not seem to be the case for those spectators who view the works as principally aesthetic objects, or as vehicles for producing in them experiences the nature of which is principally aesthetic. As certainly as we can identify the fact that some works produce in some viewers judgments of obscenity, we can identify the fact that these same works may not produce the same sorts of judgments in other viewers.

"Obscenity," or the capacity of a work to elicit a judgment that a work is obscene, seems to be relational in an interesting way. Obscenity is apparently not an intrinsic property. Without the addition of a viewer, and a viewer with individual sensibilities and a unique offense threshold, the capacity of the work for eliciting judgments of obscenity may remain unactualized. Without the viewer and her sensibilities the work in itself is neither obscene nor innocent. It is in combination with an agent that the work's capacity or power for inciting obscene or innocent reactions is actualized in any interesting way. Receptivity of viewers to the powers or capacities of the work may and do change, not only from one viewer to another, but also from one time period to another. There is no doubt that Mapplethorpe's work in the 18th or 19th centuries would have elicited a much stronger reaction from viewers. Society as a whole, at least superficially, is much more tolerant of themes that some quarters consider shocking.

Is it the case that works that do produce obscene judgments in viewers— say, on the whole or in most viewers—are *not* works of art? This does not seem to follow. Though an object may incite in a viewer many reactions— one may see it in terms of its function, say to mow a lawn or to arouse prurient interests—it does not follow that this same object cannot be viewed in such a way to produce some aesthetic reaction. That is, while some claim that Mapplethorpe's work primarily elicits judgments of obscenity, it does not follow that Mapplethorpe's work cannot also elicit aesthetic judgments.

Whatever art is, it is clear that its ability to incite reactions that are different from what we might call purely aesthetic judgments does not lessen its art status. Indeed, would Picasso's *Guernica* be as powerful aesthetically without the force of its statement about war? Would Twain's *The Adventures of Huckleberry Finn* be as aesthetically good were we to completely disregard the moral aspects of the work? It seems clear that while artworks seem principally most valuable through their ability to create in us, time and time again, rich and rewarding aesthetic reactions, it also seems the case that their ability to do so in part depends on ancillary considerations. Some of those considerations are their political statements, their moral viewpoints, and their ability to express some sexual message, such as is the case with Mapplethorpe's work, or their ability to communicate the noninviolability of any concepts, such as we see in Andres Serrano's (Serrano was at the center of a controversy for receiving NEA funding for his photograph entitled *Piss-Christ*.) work and recently in Ofili's. Thus, it follows that one cannot argue that a thing is not art *because* it is obscene. The same object may well be both obscene—in that it elicits judgments of obscenity—and an art object.

The point behind this discussion is of course to determine what ought to be done with obscene art. Surely it stands to reason that we ought to restrict obscene art from the viewing of children, at least to the degree that their parents judge them too immature to appreciate the work as art. Yet, in America we apparently value freedom of expression to a greater degree than we value avoiding offending the moral or religious sentiments of any one part of the society. If the greater value is freedom of expression, obscene art ought not be censored any more than this.

SUGGESTIONS FOR DRAWING THE LINE

To judge a work of art on purely aesthetic grounds is not to do justice to the way we really do, and seemingly must, treat art existing in a moral society. Clearly, we should not ignore the lessons that such works as *Guernica*, *The Adventures of Huckleberry Finn*, and the Judgment Scene on the altar wall of the Sistine Chapel teach. To do this would be to miss the *whole* value that such works possess. The aesthetic experience of such works is more complete when it takes into account the lessons and moral insights that are available in such works.

Consider the following suggestion: perhaps we ought to treat the evaluation of works of art as the collection of all of the points of view they possess, each of which when considered would raise the value of that work (or experience of that work)? For instance, one may have a richer experience of *Huck Finn* if she pays attention to the moral viewpoint. One may have a more rewarding experience of *Guernica* were she to know that it was in protest over the unjust bombing of a town in the Spanish Civil War.

The difficulty with such an approach, no matter how attractive it may seem, is that is fails to take account of values that, when recognized, *diminish* the experience of the artwork because they offend us morally, religiously, or otherwise. Andres Serrano's work, *Piss-Christ,* is a photograph of a crucifix suspended in a jar of urine. While the photo may be aesthetically meritorious, a viewer might find her experience of the work substantially affected. One may be quite offended by the subject matter of Serrano's work, not on aesthetic grounds, but on religious ones. This was clearly the case when Mayor Giuliani viewed Chris Ofili's work. Here the value of the experience is substantially decreased in paying attention to possible religious connotations in the work. We could adapt our definition: We should include all values as relevant that in any way contribute *or* detract from the overall experience of the work. But this of course is to say little if anything at all.

Consider a second suggestion. In spite of the fact that we have a strong belief in the freedom of expression, we as a society hold certain values still more dear than access to art. These values might include life, health (including psychological health), property, and autonomy. If *these* values come into jeopardy, in a real and tangible way, from the creation or presentation of certain artworks, then one might claim that such artworks should be censored.

In the early 1970s, Chris Burden created two interesting works of art. In one, *Shoot,* he had himself shot in the arm. In another, *Transfixed,* he had himself crucified to a Volkswagen. Should these works have been censored? Clearly he had the gun and the nails aimed at himself; had he aimed them at other people, the issue would not be a matter of censorship but of breaking the law. But since he was only harming himself, can this constitute a violation of his own rights to life and health? Or is this rather a case for respecting Burden's bodily autonomy?

More and more, graffiti is being viewed in a new light. The nighttime spray painting of young people who "tag" buildings, bridges, and cars is viewed by some as a clear example of indigenous art. Are "taggers" merely vandals? Or are they artists? Are they vandals if they exhibit their talents on property not their own? What if they paint public structures?

When I was in college I had the very good fortune to attend the Edinburgh Festival, a multiweek, high-intensity celebration of art in Edinburgh, Scotland. The festival takes place annually in late August and early September. I attended an experimental play in a very small playhouse, so small that the audience could not leave without climbing onto the stage to get out. Were we trapped? If you trap audience members, is this a violation of their rights to autonomy? Or is this justified on the grounds that they chose to attend this production, knowing they would be "captive" for the duration?

What about a violation of one's autonomy where one expects to view one thing, but the artist "imposes" another—something unwished for on the part of the viewer? In the middle of the boat scene in *Willy Wonka & the Chocolate Factory,* we see a chicken's head being cut off. This is clearly unexpected and has probably caused more than one parent some concern. There are instances aplenty where psychological harm may well be done in the viewing of an art object, either individually or—as is the frequent claim in the case of pornography—collectively as a society.

These examples demonstrate that the line between what should be censored and what should not is a fuzzy one. Given that we are in the period of great artistic challenge, the issue of what should be censored and what should not is as relevant as ever.

Judgment

CHAPTER 8

Defining "Beauty"

SECTION ONE:
WHY DEFINE "BEAUTY"?

We began the chapter on defining art with considering why we ought define 'art'. A few comments before treating the question *What is Beauty?* seem in order here. Perhaps everyone reading this is familiar with the statement that "beauty is in the eye of the beholder." We tend to infer from that statement more than simply that beauty is a subjective phenomenon. We tend to infer that what may be beautiful for one beholder may be different from what is beautiful for another beholder. Perhaps this is correct. To go one more step, perhaps there really are no criteria upon which to judge between conflicting claims that a thing is beautiful or not.

Certainly there is a great divergence in views about what is beautiful and what is not. When Americans view some of the body art practiced by women in eastern Africa, they may not find these bodily alterations beautiful. And yet the woman who does not participate in such practices may be ostracized by her peers as being not beautiful enough to find a spouse. Americans commonly do not find beautiful the results of the Chinese practice of foot binding, either. Older Americans today look at students in high school and college, amazed that the "younger generation" finds beauty in a proliferation of body piercings. When I was in college, the "older generation" found our multicolored dyed hair distinctly unbeautiful. In my classes, I frequently cite the *Mona Lisa* as a object that enjoys widespread agreement as to its beauty, but students commonly find that example useless or even ridiculous: They don't find the *Mona Lisa* very beautiful at all. Disagreement abounds.

But consider some of the implications of holding the view that beauty is merely a matter of personal opinion. First, there would be no means by which one person can say of his spouse that she is beautiful and not have that statement met with amusement, amusement that communicates either the triviality or the personalness of such a statement. If one remarks that a Monet painting is beautiful, or that a Merchant-Ivory film is a beautiful film, one ought expect that same look of amusement. If beauty is indeed in the eye of the beholder, to the end that there is no matter of fact about whether anything is indeed beautiful, then to say that something is beautiful is nothing other than to say that one *likes* whatever object is at hand, that the object is *attractive*, or that one is simply expressing the emotional or psychological state one happens to be in. It is either a personal matter, upon which there can be no discussion, or it is a trivial matter, given that the statement that something is beautiful is nothing other than a report of one's own exclusively personal state. Relegating beauty to the eye of the beholder, such that no beholder's judgment is any better than any other beholder's, may be to dismiss the power of claiming a thing to be beautiful. No discussion can ensue, because there would be no fact of the matter upon which to argue.

Another implication of such a position is that art evaluation, in the form of published art criticism, becomes a matter of one person (the critic) announcing personal, and in principle unsubstantiable, opinions. This holds true in other similar cases: If beauty is a matter of personal opinion, then one cannot claim that the government ought (or ought not) be spending tax dollars on the funding of projects that the government, or a group of government officials, has decided are beautiful. The same story could be told about the curator of a museum, the owner of a gallery, the buyer of art objects for public buildings, and so forth. If there is no standard of beauty, no fact of the matter, *no matter at all*, then all those judgments of beauty in objects become either trivial or personal.

On the other hand, perhaps "beauty is in the eye of the beholder" is not mean to convey that one's person's view is as good as another's. In that case, such a theory is not without its proponents. David Hume argues in favor of a certain "eye-of-the-beholder" theory. However, Hume, unlike proponents of a more relativist stance, holds that some beholders can be wrong in their assessments of whether a thing is beautiful, that there is a criteria that we apply to beholders to separate those with worthy judgments from those without.

It is the more common position to expect that when someone says that a thing is beautiful, she means to be saying something real about the object. She means to be offering a judgment that is at least meant to recommend to another viewer that he will find the object in question beautiful, too. Those who claim that a thing is beautiful are usually willing to back up their claim, defending it by citing evidence. This suggests that these people do not buy the position that claiming something is beautiful is nothing other than merely expressing a personal opinion.

There are those who claim that a thing is beautiful, but when met with resistance immediately back off their claim, reverting to "well, everyone's entitled to his opinion." But this may well be explained in terms of an avoidance of controversy or an avoidance of being called upon to give evidence and argument. When such a person meets *agreement*, rather than disagreement, he probably will feel confident that he saw in the object some real property, and he will gain confidence in his judgment from the agreement of the other person.

Relegating claims of beauty to personal opinion tends to be something that academics engage in more than "regular" people. "Regular" people mean something when they claim that a thing is beautiful. Academics, however, after a long and tiring search for what that something is, in the face of lots of divergent views, may tend to settle for the "personal opinion" route. But this does not mean that the search for the meaning of "beauty" is ultimately fruitless or useless. Quite the contrary. If general, nontheoretical common opinion is that beauty means something, then the search for a definition is not a waste of time; it is doing our best to make sense of human experience.

BEAUTY AND AESTHETIC GOODNESS

In discussing beauty, we will also be discussing aesthetic goodness. These are different things, yet closely related. Both have to do with making final judgments about the worth of aesthetic objects. But as there are objects we commonly may describe as beautiful but not aesthetically good, and objects we would describe having aesthetic merit but not beauty, some account of the difference between these two judgments is necessary.

'Aesthetically good' applies to those objects that we would not describe as beautiful, but still would, from an aesthetic point of view, praise. A good example is Francis Ford Coppola's 1979 film, *Apocalypse Now*. One may not describe *Apocalypse* as beautiful, but it is a very good film, and it deserves as high praise as anything one would consider to be very beautiful—such as Merchant-Ivory's film *Howard's End*.

Some believe that the word 'beauty' should cover the gamut. 'Beauty' should serve to describe works that are both beautiful *and* aesthetically good. They would describe both Merchant-Ivory's and Coppola's work as beautiful, because they use the word beauty to cover both sides: what one may call 'beautiful' and 'aesthetically good'. However, this seems to muddle the use of the term 'beautiful'. Since we rate these objects on apparently different criteria, why not use different terms?

A possibility is the following. When one talks of something being beautiful, she means that it is very pleasing to the senses, and perhaps pleasing in an immediate way that takes little cognitive or temporal development. When one talks of something as aesthetically good, she means that it is fulfilling, uplifting, rewarding, and so forth. Generally, this is not a mere sensory or perceptual judgment; judging something to be aesthetically good takes time and consideration. Without the consideration process, one does not appreciate the object fully.

So far it seems as if it is better to be aesthetically good than beautiful. However, the two notions are more like opposite sides of a coin than they are rivals. Beauty may be a certain pleasure or attractiveness that is taken or found in a given object in an immediate perceptual way. A judgment of aesthetic goodness is a more developed, considered appreciation or enjoyment of the object. If this distinction is correct, then 'beauty' and 'aesthetic goodness' are close cousins, with the difference being primarily a temporal or developmental one. Now, not all works that are *merely* beautiful or *merely* aesthetically good are worse than works that are both beautiful and aesthetically good. The two judgments are not additive in this way. They describe different aspects of the object. So in the final analysis they are not at all rivals, but two different ways of appreciating objects.

SECTION TWO: FORMALISM

The Formalist Theory of Beauty is distinct from the Formalist Theory of Art. For instance, while Plato and Aristotle worked with the Representation/Imitation Theory of Art, their views on what makes something beautiful or aesthetically good fall roughly into the *Formalist* Theory of Beauty. One can believe that works of art are so because they imitate other objects. They might also believe that what makes them beautiful or good lies in the arrangement or presence of certain properties.

When Sam sees a statue of a person, say of George Washington, he calls it art because it represents a famous figure in American history. Now, Sam can judge whether it is a good work of art on the same criteria—that is, Sam may say it is good because it looks much like Washington and because it portrays Washington's attitude the way Sam believes the attitude of one of the principal founders of the country should be portrayed. But Sam might also consider whether the object is beautiful or good based not on the fact that it accurately or faithfully represents it subject. He may judge the statue on the basis of formal qualities such as the balance exhibited in the statue, the elegance of the lines, the stability the composition portrays, and so forth. *Formal* qualities refer to qualities of the *form* of the object, on whether certain things like balance or elegance are present. And these properties, in turn, depend on the arrangement of certain lines, shapes, colors, tones, and so forth (what some theorists call base properties).

On the other hand, the converse of the situation with Plato and Aristotle should also be noted: it is regularly the case that when a philosopher advances a particular theory of what makes something art, her account about what makes something *good* art may be connected. For instance, Clive Bell holds that what makes a thing art is that it contains Significant Form, which when viewed attentively produces a certain aesthetic feeling in audience members. For Bell, what would make a thing a *good* work of art may be explained on similar lines: A *good* work of art is a work that has *a substantial degree* of Significant Form. Either it has a large quantity of Significant Form, or it more readily and more intensely brings out the aesthetic feeling in audiences.

It is clear why many theories of art lend themselves to explaining why things are beautiful. But consider this: theories of beauty, in most formulations, do not apply *only* to art objects. Many beauty theories apply also to natural objects, such as sunsets and ocean views, trees and flowers, cats and horses. Not only do these theories cover why paintings and symphonies are beautiful—that is, *if* they are beautiful—but they also explain why (some) sunsets and flowers are beautiful. The Formalist Theory of Beauty, depending on the particular theory being discussed, may fit into any of the categories broadly described above. The Beauty-Formalist may

(1) have his Theory of Art dictate his Theory of Beauty,

(2) have his Beauty Theory and his Art Theory be at odds, perhaps because his Beauty Theory is designed to cover sunsets and flowers, too, or

(3) have no Theory of Art at all, but be simply interested in beauty, in how objects are aesthetically good (because sunsets and flowers, like paintings and films, can be aesthetically good or bad or somewhere in between), and in how we know whether objects are beautiful or aesthetically good.

It will depend on which theory we are discussing as to which of the above three scenarios fit.

PLATO

Recollect Plato's theory of art. For Plato, art is removed from reality because art is merely an imitation of physical or natural objects, and physical objects are imitations of the Forms, or essences. Now, one of the Platonic Forms is itself Beauty. So it follows that what is beautiful is what participates in the Form of Beauty. And what is *most* beautiful, or *truly* beautiful, is that Form itself, and so through contemplation of the Form of Beauty we come to truly know beauty. In a dialogue between Socrates and Diotima in his *Symposium*, Plato tells us that knowledge of beauty is a process that begins through the appreciation of objects in the natural world. First, we appreciate individual human bodies. Then we appreciate the human body, finding beauty in various bodies, and then in all beautiful bodies. Next we move toward an appreciation of abstract concepts. We appreciate that true human beauty is not bodily but in the soul. Then we appreciate the "laws and institutions" that order human society, says Plato. From there we appreciate the beauty of knowledge, and of every type of knowledge. From this point we are able to appreciate the Forms themselves, and when we have matured aesthetically, we finally appreciate the Form of Beauty.

Plato holds that art itself was potentially valueless because (1) it is removed from reality, (2) it pretended to express some knowledge, which in actuality it could not do, (3) it is sensual and true beauty is spiritual, and (4) it appeals to the appetitive side of the soul, not to the rational side. However, *if* certain artworks could serve a need or had a practical purpose, then they might be redeemable. If art is to have any value, says Plato, it must support the society or state. The value that art has is not an aesthetic value, or a pedagogical value (that it might teach something). A work of art, if it has any value, has *political* value in its support of the state. It serves a purpose by teaching virtues, by celebrating the old heroes, and by praising the goodness of the gods. It ought to show not frailties but only strengths. It must not show cowardice but only bravery. It must show no weakness. This means that art such as tragedy, which focuses on the flaws of persons, is *not* a good artform. Furthermore, artforms that seek to evoke emotions are also bad. Dramatic art, which might make us cry or be overly introspectful or somber, is a bad artform. Only celebratory artforms are valuable, and they are valuable only through their ability to teach us to aspire to become greater ourselves, become more contemplative, or become a more ardent member of the society. So, for an object to be beautiful is for that object to

(1) be an object that participates in the Form of Beauty, and the closer the relationship is between the Form and the beauty in the object, the more beautiful is the object.

However, for an object to be an *aesthetically good object* is for that object to

(1) be an art object, and
(2) support the state by contributing to the virtues of the citizenry and their appreciation of the virtues in others, such as in the heroes and gods.

Now, there are still theories that promote ideas much like Plato's. Recall the case of Tolstoy, who says art is meant to support the religious climate of the society in which it is created. If it fails to do this, it is bad art.

ARISTOTLE

Aristotle's view of beauty and aesthetic goodness, like his theory of art, is markedly different from Plato's. But to begin, we will discuss a similarity to Plato. Like Plato, Aristotle has two separate things to say about what makes objects beautiful or good. The content of those two things, however, distinguishes Aristotle from Plato. First is his account of goodness, and second is the set of specific items he says contribute to beauty or goodness in objects.

Aristotle's theory of goodness, whether in aesthetics or in any other field where value judgments are made, has come to be known as the *Functional Account of Goodness*. This Functional Account states that for a thing to be good, that object must

(1) function highly as an instance of the kind under which it is being considered.

This definition works not only for questions typically considered to be in value disciplines like aesthetics or ethics, but also for any use of the term 'good'. For example, for a knife to be a good knife is for it to cut well, and, objectively, it will be a good knife if it is sharp, strong, and so forth. Apparently, one could object that to be a hunting knife is to be different from a butter knife. And the Aristotelian analysis adapts: For an object to be a good hunting knife is for it to be sharp, strong, large, and pointed, and for an object to be a good butter knife is for it to be delicate, easily held, well balanced, and rounded on the end.

The Functional Account can also be applied to art: For an object to be a *good* art object is for it to fulfill the function of what it is to be an art object to a high degree. If you recall the Aristotelian analysis of what it is to be an art object, the account of what it is to be a good art object is for that object to

(1) be an artifact,

(2) imitate the universal or archetypal in nature,

(3) delight viewers (hearers and so forth), and

(4) fulfill these criteria—at least (2) and (3)—to a high degree. The function of art—
its ultimate end—is expressed in (1), (2), and (3). So art that fulfills its function is
good art.

It would have been quite odd for Aristotle, who was interested in nature, to
fail to account for aesthetically good *natural* objects. Though strictly a functional account can be applied to any value judgment, we would need a definition of what it is to be an *aesthetic object*—not just an *art* object—before we
could apply a functional account. That is, though the definitions of items
designed for some particular use can readily be identified (a knife is, more or
less, for cutting), there is no *obvious* or uncontentious definition for what
makes an aesthetic object an aesthetic object. Moreover, if we simply wish to
adjust the above art-analysis, the only two tenets that survive are (3) and (4).
So for an object to be a good aesthetic object is for it to

(A) delight viewers (hearers and so forth) and

(B) fulfill (A) to a high degree.

This seems to be a weak analysis, because there seem to be many objects that
do in fact delight us, and do so to a high degree, but that we do not normally
appreciate aesthetically. An example is cake and ice cream. Unless we first
construct a story in which cake and ice cream are appreciated *aesthetically*,
then cake and ice cream are not fine examples of aesthetic objects, no matter
how delightful they are. One may be delighted in their consumption, but they
are not appreciated in the same way that one would appreciate a lovely sunset
or a Monet.

Aristotle needed to identify what it is about objects that we appreciate when
we appreciate them *aesthetically*, in this aesthetic analysis, we come to his second, *and clearly Formalist*, analysis. Aristotle said that the most important elements in a consideration of whether something is beautiful are (1) order,
(2) symmetry and (3) definiteness. If an object exhibits these elements to a
high degree, then we can correctly say that this object is beautiful. If the
object is well ordered, highly symmetrical, and bounded and we experience a
closure or sense of completion and, as Aristotle put it, *definiteness*—then that
object cannot fail to be beautiful. So for an object to be beautiful, or aesthetically good, is for that object to

(1) be ordered,

(2) be symmetrical,

(3) be definite, and

(4) meet each of these criteria to a high degree.

It is important to see here that Aristotle offers a *formula* by offering *principles* for what constitutes necessary and sufficient conditions for something being beautiful. ('Formula' will be used to specify some set of formal characteristics that must be objectively present for a thing to be beautiful or good.) This program of offering principles of beauty endures throughout the history and discipline of aesthetics. If we can find a formula for determining what constitutes beauty, then we are in a better position on two counts: (1) we can more precisely criticize works against that criterion, and artists can aim toward inclusion of those elements in order to ensure that their works are truly beautiful. (2) The entire task can be done objectively, from the vantage point of present, observable, and easily accessible characteristics of objects. This can be done without bias.

Unfortunately, no formula, no set of aesthetic principles ever offered has either met with a pre-existent apparent counterexample or has had an apparent counterexample created soon after that defeats it. That is, whatever formula we fashion or advocate, we must be aware that it must fit all of the objects in the world that are determined, *without benefit of the formula*, to be beautiful. The formula must fit our *intuitions* of what is beautiful, and the set of objects we believe to be beautiful might be a very large set indeed. This is an initial problem. However, another problem seems always to follow: once a formula is put forward, it is almost always (1) met with some artist's creation that we believe to be beautiful, but apparently fails to meet our analysis, or (2) met with some object that apparently fulfills the criterion completely but fails to be beautiful.

In a real sense, we *know* what it is for an object to be beautiful, because even without having touched an aesthetics book or philosophized about beauty at all, we commonly utter such as "My, that's a beautiful sunset" or "I've never seen such a beautiful rose." The trick then is to come up with an analysis of what it is to be beautiful that can capture all of our intuitions about beauty. As it was with Aristotle, to give this analysis *may* be to give a formula. However, it is difficult, to say the least, to specify what principles must be instantiated for something to be beautiful. This is why formulas such as Aristotle's are commonly rejected. All we need do is find one object that is beautiful but fails to be ordered, symmetrical, or definite. Or all we need do is find an object that is ordered, symmetrical, and definite, but *fails* to be beautiful, and the proposed account is in trouble.

While Aristotle's analysis of what makes something beautiful may come up lacking, two lessons are learned from his work. First, one way to determine what is beautiful is to offer a formula, where if certain criteria are met, the object in question is beautiful, and if the object fails to be beautiful, it is because it is lacking in one of the criteria. However, this road has problems. So the second lesson we learn is that instead of asking whether something really is beautiful, which seems to invite a formula-analysis, we might instead ask how we *know* whether objects are beautiful or not. If it is true that "beauty is in the eye of the beholder," then perhaps we ought focus less on the object in question and more on the beholder. We will see in many of the following analyses that *both* of these roads are followed.

LORD SHAFTESBURY

Anthony Ashley Cooper, the third earl of Shaftesbury, used *both* analyses, the one regarding whether something really is beautiful and the other regarding how we know it is beautiful. Shaftesbury was a Platonist, which means in part that he believed that there was a real property or essence of beauty that existed apart from particular beautiful objects. Beautiful objects are objects that participate in that essence of beauty. The question, then, is how we come to *know* that some object is indeed participating in that beauty-essence. Shaftesbury is credited as being the first aesthetician to use the notion of *disinterest* as a way to determine how we know whether something is beautiful. Shaftesbury thought that if we viewed something disinterestedly—that is, divorcing ourselves from self-interests and disregarding any benefit the object may afford us—then we would be in the proper mental position to correctly determine whether that object was indeed beautiful. Shaftesbury held that there is such a thing as the supersensible essence of beauty and that we can know whether an object participates in this essence if we will only view it disinterestedly. He believed that we all have something he called the *Moral Sense*, an inward eye that immediately grasps rightness and beauty. This Moral Sense constitutes, in part, the faculty of *taste*, or the ability to discern the beautiful. In aesthetic judgments, this inward eye identifies or is inspired by the property of beauty in an object. If one's perception or attitude is one of disinterest, the Moral Sense will pick out beauty in the object.

Unlike Plato, however, Shaftesbury continues his analysis by telling us what *natural properties* must be in an object to make it beautiful. Shaftesbury offers us a formula. If an object is beautiful, then it must and does possess the formal quality of *unity-in-multiplicity*. We view the object with disinterest, and if after taking on this initial attitude, we perceive this unity-in-multiplicity, then we can correctly assert that the object is beautiful. Unity-in-multiplicity is something like seeing many aspects to the object, a certain complexity, but also seeing an order, structure, or theme that binds them all together. But unity-in-multiplicity, as an analysis, certainly seems open to interpretation.

Shaftesbury offers us a double-barreled approach to beauty. First, we must be in a certain state or attitude, or *correctly disposed*, in order to be appropriately receptive to seeing the property of beauty in objects. Second, once we are in that disinterested state, we will be able to determine whether an object is beautiful on the basis of whether it possesses unity-in-multiplicity. If it does, then it is beautiful. If not, then it is not beautiful. So for an object to be beautiful is for that object to

(1) be considered with a disinterested attitude, and

(2) participate in the essence of beauty, which is to possess the formal property of unity-in-multiplicity.

At first, we might wish to ask (1) whether there are any objects that are beautiful that do not have unity-in-multiplicity, or (2) whether there are any objects that have unity-in-multiplicity but that still are not beautiful. If we can find any, then one of two things must be the case. Either the object is really not beautiful, or we are failing to view disinterestedly. If we are in the correct frame of mind and we still observe that (1) or (2) is the case, then we have to question the correctness of Shaftesbury's analysis of beauty.

Consider the work of Jackson Pollock. Any one of Pollock's later works, supposing it to be beautiful, may be a perfect example of unity-in-multiplicity. If a Pollock work were considered not beautiful and we were viewing disinterestedly, then we might make a case on that basis for rejecting Shaftesbury's account. Consider the sky. The sky, say on a cloudless day, is beautiful. But it does not exhibit multiplicity. Shaftesbury proponents might argue that it does however exhibit an extraordinary degree of unity, such that the unity overtakes, as the criterion of beauty, the multiplicity. While the cloudless sky is quite unified, the account still reads unity-*in-multiplicity*.

Once we begin to adjust the formula, as in this last example, we run the danger of watering down the account with excessive interpretation of the analysis. If we water down the analysis so far that any counterexample, no matter how apparent, can be explained away, then the analysis ceases to function in the way it was meant to. If we are in the position of making *any* object fit the criterion of unity-in-multiplicity, then the account fails on grounds of uselessness.

FRANCIS HUTCHESON

Francis Hutcheson repeated to a large extent what Shaftesbury had said, especially with regard to disinterest. There are, however, differences significant enough to include Hutcheson in our review. First and foremost, Hutcheson was not a Platonist. He did not believe that the property or essence of beauty existed outside of beautiful objects. However, as did Shaftesbury, he offered a double-barreled analysis. First, one must, as with Shaftesbury, adopt the attitude of disinterest in order to properly judge. And like Shaftesbury, consonant with this attitude was a certain natural faculty that we each possess. Unlike the faculty of the Moral Sense, Hutcheson's faculty was more physiologically based. His was a faculty like that of sight or hearing. This is the faculty of taste, and Hutcheson called it the *Internal Sense*. The Internal Sense was, for Hutcheson, as real and present as any other sensory faculty, though one cannot physically locate any *taste-organ* as one could locate the eyes or ears.

As humans—that is, those with "working" senses—see something red and rather quickly agree that the color is indeed red, so it is that when we see in objects that which triggers the Internal Sense we immediately see, and subsequently agree, that this object is indeed beautiful. First, we must understand that just as with eyes and ears, we must have senses that work. And they not only have to work, but they also have to be *practiced* and sensitive. For instance, Sally may tell the difference between red and orange, but she might have a difficult time telling the difference between lavender and lilac as shades of light purple. She may not be practiced enough. So it is with viewing aesthetic objects. We must be practiced in viewing aesthetics objects in order to determine whether they are beautiful. If we are not practiced, then we may not be able to tell the difference in borderline cases of beauty.

Second, like Shaftesbury, Hutcheson offers a formula for determining what objects are beautiful. For Hutcheson what triggers the Internal Sense is uniformity-amongst-variety. For an object to be beautiful is for that object to

(1) be considered from a disinterested attitude, and

(2) possess the formal property of uniformity-amongst-variety.

As with Shaftesbury's analysis, uniformity-amongst-variety is open to some interpretation. *Over*interpretation is a danger. If we do not overinterpret, then Hutcheson's account based on uniformity-amongst-variety is susceptible to the same attacks as Shaftesbury's. Supposing that we are in the correct attitude of disinterest, are there objects that either (1) are beautiful but do not exhibit uniformity-amongst-variety or (2) are not beautiful but *do* exhibit uniformity-amongst-variety?

Lord Shaftesbury and Francis Hutcheson are but two of the several philosophers in the 18th century, in the tradition of British Empiricism, who advocated the *aesthetic attitude* of disinterest. For us to correctly determine whether something is beautiful, we must be in a certain frame of mind. This we discussed in chapter 2.

MONROE C. BEARDSLEY

We discussed two ancient Greek views, those of Plato and of Aristotle, and we have discussed two 18th-century views, those of Shaftesbury and Hutcheson. Beardsley, however, is a Beauty-Formalist who is quite contemporary (he died in 1985). In his discussion of beauty and/or aesthetic goodness, Beardsley's focus is not the aesthetic object per se, but rather the *aesthetic experience*. He particularly focuses on the relationship between the perceiver and the object. This is important because it pushes the Formalist character of Beardsley's analysis from being strictly about the object to being about *both* the object and the experience of the perceiver. In fact, the measure of how much beauty or goodness is present is not merely through an appraisal of the object. It is through a measure of the mental processes that happen when the viewer focuses on the formal characteristics of the object. This is similar to the phenomenon described by Clive Bell. The gratification felt when the viewer focuses on the formal qualities of the object is, for Beardsley, the measure of how good or beautiful the object is. This is the aesthetic experience: that the viewer's attention is focused on the formal qualities of the object, and her psychological state is characterized by *unity and pleasure.*

There is a mutual relationship between the formal qualities of the object and the mental state of the viewer. The object is measured against three criteria regarding its formal qualities: (1) unity, (2) intensity, and (3) complexity. When the attending viewer's mental state is also unified—and/or intense, and/or complex—and is made pleasurable through paying attention to the object, then the object may be said to be truly beautiful or aesthetically good. For an object to be an aesthetically good object is for it to

(1) be unified, and/or intense, and/or complex (natural formal qualities), and

(2) be such that it prompts in attentive perceivers a pleasurable experience characterized by unity, and/or intensity, and/or complexity.

FORMALISM CONSIDERED

In each of the Formalist analyses, we see how it is through the formal qualities of the object that the beauty or aesthetic goodness of the object is discovered. Each account—with the exception of Plato—offers a set of criteria or a formula to determine whether something is beautiful and/or aesthetically good. If an object possesses certain formal properties or a certain *arrangement* of *base properties* (base properties are properties such as shape, color, and line), then that object is beautiful or good. If it fails to possess these properties or their proper arrangement, then it fails to be beautiful or good.

Beyond the offerings of these formulas, many of the Formalists suggest that we must be in a certain frame of mind to appreciate properly. Many of the 18th-century British aestheticians believe we must be disinterested in order to appropriately judge whether something is beautiful. Beardsley believes that the necessary disposition comes not at the beginning of perceiving the object, but *through* perceiving the object; our mental activity is made pleasurable and unified/intense/complex on the basis of our perceiving those same characteristics in the object itself.

One interesting item is that since the 18th-century Formalists, we have progressed from a more objectivist account of what makes a thing beautiful toward a more *relational* account. In a relational account, the perceiver has some responsibility, either in actualizing the beauty or in being in the proper state to know that the object is beautiful. This bears similarities to the Formalist Theory of *Art*. Although Formalism has as its initial motivation to center upon the objective characteristics of the object itself to determine the object's status—either as art or as possessor of beauty—the trend has been to move to a greater inclusion of the viewer and her mental state.

SECTION THREE: SUBJECTIVISM

THE STANDARD OF TASTE: THE VIEW OF DAVID HUME

David Hume is one of the most popular philosophers of all time. Although his reputation has been made through his discussions of other topics, his views on aesthetics have been influential as well. Hume seeks not to answer questions about whether something truly is beautiful or good. He concentrates on the possibility of our *knowing* whether something is beautiful. That is, he focuses on the role of the evaluator.

Hume begins with the now-famous statement: "de gustibus non disputandum est"—loosely translated, "There is no disputing taste." If the appreciation of an object brings us pleasure, then how can we be wrong about that? One cannot be talked out of *liking* what she likes. How one *feels* may not be open for rational discussion. We may be able to inquire into the causes of feelings or likes, but we cannot, through *simple* rational discourse, *affect* those feelings or likes. This is Hume's starting place; he writes "all sentiment is right; because sentiment has a reference to nothing beyond itself" (from "Of the Standard of Taste").

Suppose Sam and Sally are walking down the street, and Sam points out something in a store window that strikes him as attractive. Sally disagrees and attempts to argue Sam out of his belief. She may say, "Look at that shabby workmanship; look at how the colors clash." But in spite of all her talk, Sam is still attracted to the object. Perhaps Sam could be wrong in whether the object is truly beautiful or aesthetically good, but can we honestly say that Sam ought not *like* it? By understanding the incorrigibility (not open to correction) of likes and dislikes, and by understanding that this is really the starting point when it comes to our aesthetic judgments, Hume sets the stage for his account.

Now, merely because one likes a certain object, this is not to say that the object is indeed beautiful or aesthetically good. Those two states are different: One is a simple immediate psychological state; the second is an aesthetic judgment that in some measure must be able to be defended and supported. When we say that something is beautiful or good, we are not merely declaring that we like it; we are *asserting a certain judgment*. We are evaluating the object. When we say, "That object is beautiful," we are saying something that refers the way the world really is, to a matter of *fact*, that is to say, whether the object is indeed beautiful. Hume says that though our feelings are pertinent in our aesthetic judgments—they are the starting place—they do not tell the whole story. The whole story must include the realization that when we make an aesthetic judgment, we *mean* to be saying something that is *true* or *false* and open to discussion and revision. If we simply reduce our aesthetic judgments to our likes and dislikes, then the concept of beauty does not *mean* the same thing as the way we *normally* use the word. We normally use the word to assert a statement that we believe can be right or wrong. "No, that's not beautiful. In fact, it's quite awful," Sally might say in response to Sam's assertion that the object in the store window is beautiful. This is meaningful only if there is something *outside ourselves* to which we refer when we assert that something is beautiful. The Humean account, then, is not pure subjectivism. While it is a form of "beauty is in the eye of the beholder," it does not go on to say "and one beholder's eye is as good as another's."

Some forms or qualities, Hume states in his essay, "Of the Standard of Taste," seem *calculated to please or to displease*. There are patterns to what we commonly take to be beautiful objects or ugly objects, and there are properties present in these objects that lie at the heart of these patterns. However, once that is said, we might expect Hume to offer an objective formula. He does not. Instead, he begins to develop a set of *rules of judgment* that are found through experience.

So far this may not sound different from the offering of an objective formula. However, instead of looking to the object for determining the constitution of beauty, he looks to the audience member or the judge. The rules, if they are discoverable through experience, are found in the judgments of individuals *and are about these judgments*. So instead of studying the object of the judgment, Hume elects to study the judgments themselves. What he seeks to understand are the patterns of common sentiments. If we all like or dislike similar things, then it is *these* patterns that need investigation. Moreover, there is ample evidence that we like and dislike similarly; this is the evidence that allows Hume to say that some qualities are *calculated* to please and some not.

The problem, unfortunately, is that these patterns are not stable, lasting, and fool-proof. There will be occasions when we disagree about what might on the surface seem obvious examples of beautiful objects. Sam may believe Monet's *Water Lilies* to be obviously beautiful, but Sally may not. Or there will be occasions when objects rest on a boundary between beauty and ordinariness. These hard cases provide reason for keeping the judgment rules that we develop sufficiently loose (perhaps even too loose to function to determine correct judgments from incorrect ones, but this remains to be seen).

Hume introduces a means to address the disagreement problem. If we could find someone who was in the position to generally provide correct beauty judgments, then instead of taking a poll each time we want to determine whether something is beautiful (and polls are pretty wishy-washy devices anyhow), we could appeal to the judgment of our special critic, our *true judge*. For an object to be a beautiful and/or aesthetically good object is for it to

(1) provoke aesthetic sentiment in appropriately disposed competent critics, in *true judges*.

Now the problem is to find these *true judges*. Hume suggests that the qualities of such judges include:

(A) that they have a serenity of mind (this is mentioned earlier in "Of the Standard of Taste" than the other five),

(B) that they have a delicacy of taste,

(C) that they are well practiced,

(D) that they are versed in comparison between objects,

(E) that they are free from prejudice, and

(F) that they have good sense (or that their senses work very well).

Judges who have at least these characteristics are the judges, then, who we can appeal to in the determination of whether some object is actually beautiful. If they are inspired to *like* the object, given their backgrounds and special natures, then the object is indeed beautiful.

Unfortunately, the *true judge* account is not free from difficulties. First, it may be that in order for Hume to be correct, it ought to be the case that in all of aesthetic study, a set of principles which confer aesthetic merit—a true *objective* formula—ought to have been drawn up. That is, if we can find patterns among judgments, we ought to be able to identify the objective properties that give rise to these judgments. If particular properties present in objects account for the similarity of judgment, then it is reasonable to expect that throughout time they could have been identified and written down. Some might answer that such principles—which a position like Hume's would suggest—are *logically* identifiable, but because of the almost infinite variety of things that we consider beautiful, this list is simply too complex to be drawn up. There is a logical possibility of such a list, but the probability of actually identifying it is very low.

Second, some criticize that no *true judge* actually seems to exist. This leads to the question about whether there could *really* be such a judge. However, the fact that something does not exist does not mean that it cannot. Our *true judge* would have to have some extraordinary properties whose presence all together in one person might be extraordinary. However, there is nothing that would *logically* preclude the existence of such a person. Moreover, we may be happy enough to have the *true judge* serve just as a sort of "ideal" standard—not a real person, but a goal at which to aim in establishing the criteria for making good aesthetic judgments.

Another criticism of *true judge* theories in general is that we tend, in the description of our *true judge*, to build in just those attributes that we ourselves believe would contribute to her ability to judge correctly. We tend to make our *true judge* in our own image. This, it seems, given that we ourselves are not *true judges*, defeats the project. Once we found a single other aesthetician who believed that the *true judge* would have different attributes from the ones with which we endow him, the problem that the *true judge* theory was supposed to solve returns. How is it that we establish the features of the *true judge*? If it is through a consensus of opinion, then we might as well "cut out the middleman" and seek majority opinions directly about which objects are beautiful. As it stands, Hume's list seems obvious enough, and perhaps it is in the end the better strategy to try to find commonality among a list of true-judge properties rather than look for something else that can be found to be common among aesthetic judgments.

Finally, what about the possibility of irreconcilable differences between *true judges*? Suppose that Sam and Sally, each equally and well qualified to be *true judges* and each appropriately disposed, were to judge an object. Sam determines that the object is not beautiful, but Sally says that the object is. How can the Humean account solve such a problem? Hume does say in "Of the Standard of Taste" that "the joint verdict of [*true judges*] ... is the true standard of taste and beauty." However, what if the judgments of two *true judges* were incompatible? What if they were so inconsistent that no joint verdict were possible? To answer that such a thing could not happen would seem to go against the empirical character of how Hume determines which judgments are correct and which are not. The problem of the possibility of conflicting judgments between *true judges* is the most difficult of the lot.

If any of these questions in unanswerable by Hume's theory, then the *true judge* theory of establishing what is beautiful or aesthetically good may suffer. Of the criticisms, the strongest is the possibility of incompatible and irreconcilable differences between *true judges*. If this were to occur, we would then need to look for some analysis of how we might decide which of the two ideal judges is correct. In other words, the *true judge* theory would not be doing its job. The difficulty is brought home when we reflect on the number of art critics working today and the fact that they disagree more than agree. If we allow our best art critics (those whose qualities most closely match Hume's list) to act as our *true judges*, then we immediately see the strength of the difficulty of competing views. Art critics disagree with one another. They disagree a lot.

UNIVERSALITY: THE VIEW OF IMMANUEL KANT

Kant's position in aesthetics, much like other of his positions, may best be understood against the backdrop of Hume's position. As we saw, Hume's view attempts to capture the authority and diversity of the individual aesthetic judgment, while also attempting to account for our belief that some judgments are true and some are false. Though Hume's account handles the toughest problems that face the empiricist aesthetician, he does not advance a criterion for right judgments apart from his trust in the judgments of the *true judges*. It is from this point that Kant begins to explore how it is that we can account for similarity among judgments about what objects are beautiful and/or aesthetically good. If this can be discovered, then we have a basis for establishing the rightness or wrongness of aesthetic judgments and can still keep our subjectivist ("eye-of-the-beholder") focus.

Kant begins by stating that when we judge an object to be beautiful—just a single object, like a rose we see one day—we expect and demand that others will judge that particular object just as we do. This expectation, or demand, for similarity is what fuels Kant's search for some explanation of the similarity between the aesthetic judgments of various viewers.

First off, Kant is talking only about a single judgment: a particular judgment about (say) a particular rose. This effectively eliminates the possibility of offering objective formulas for beauty. Formulas would range over objects that share similar characteristics. Kant denies this possibility: No rules or principles of taste are possible, he says.

Second, in talking about the expectation of similarity, Kant is not discussing what he calls judgments of agreeableness. *Judgments of agreeableness* are about likes and dislikes. In talking about an expectation of similarity, Kant is referring to a similarity about *judgments of taste* or aesthetic judgments. These judgments, he says in concert with Hume, seem to have a deeper ground that mere likes and dislikes. They refer to the way the world really is, to a matter of fact. Judgments of taste must be defended apart from pure sentiment.

This is not to say that sentiment—likes and dislikes—do not play a role. As they do with Hume, they do with Kant. But Kant sees sentiment as playing only a partial role. Sentiment is part of what makes up our aesthetic judgment—it has to be, says Kant, because if it were not, then aesthetic judgments would be purely rational judgments and would be as subject to logical scrutiny as any other purely rational judgments. However, sentiment is not the only part. The cognitive plays a role, too. Kant describes the cognitive part as the "free play between the understanding and the imagination."

Since the aesthetic judgment is a complex of cognition and sentiment, it is not open to the logical exploration that purely cognitive judgments are. The aesthetic judgment is not, says Kant, a matter for the logician. The aesthetic judgment is properly described as being a purely *subjective* judgment. This is to say that the judgment is in the eye of the beholder; however, *this is not to say that the judgment may differ from one beholder to another.* And the ground of the similarity—of the universality of aesthetic judgments—is and must be purely subjective, too. But how can a judgment made by an individual subject be universal with respect to the aesthetic judgments of everyone else?

This is the tough question. If Sam judges a particular rose to be beautiful, and Sally judges it not to be beautiful, then how are we supposed to come to agreement if our judgments are purely subjective? All we have to go on is this abiding expectation (or demand) for agreement. We do not base the search for similarity on the fact that people actually agree; to do this is to take the purely empirical route, and Kant thought that was a mistake. (This is where we see the greatest divergence between Kant's theory and Hume's.) The expectation that we agree comes not because we *do* agree; the expectation comes because we *must* agree. If the aesthetic judgment is to make sense, it must be universal, thought Kant.

Aesthetic judgments are not purely cognitive—because if they were we would not be faced with such hard problems. We would simply use the logic that governs correct reasoning to determine correct judgments. But aesthetic judgments are not purely sentimental. If they were, we would not be able to move beyond Hume's problem of the *authority* of sentimental judgments of likes and dislikes. So Kant says that the universality, which we must absolutely have to make sense of aesthetic judgments, must be a combination of cognition and sentiment. Moreover, the universality or agreement among aesthetic judgment is due, he says, to our having a *common sense*. This is not "common sense" in the way we think of *practicality*. It is a complex ability to identify the beauty or aesthetic goodness of an individual object.

Part of the key to this turns on the physical and mental similarities among human beings. The similarity between the judgments of various agents is expected because, in part, the cognitive part of our judgments is similar. Since aesthetic judgment is not merely a matter of sentiment, but a matter of what Kant calls free play between the understanding and the imagination, and the aesthetic judgment is cognitive *as well as* sentimental, we can go a long way in explaining why we *would* judge similarly. We have similar *cognitive* structures, so even though we all have different likes and dislikes, we can understand why we would come up with similar aesthetic judgments.

But how do we account for differences among our likes and dislikes? If we are all built alike, why do we have separate likes and dislikes? This may be because we have different experiences, different biases and partialities, different educational levels, different levels of exposure to art or aesthetic objects, different maturity levels, and perhaps even different sensory abilities.

Kant offers us a way to try to *reconcile* our likes and dislikes with other aesthetic judges. It is based on *disinterest*. It is important for a judge to be in the proper frame of mind for making an aesthetic judgment, and the proper disposition is for the judge to be disinterested. This is similar to the views of Shaftesbury and Hutcheson. Given disinterest on the part of the judge, and given that we all have similar faculties for understanding the world *and* for making subjective judgments, *we would all judge similarly*. At least, says Kant, we would all judge similarly *in singular judgments*: "this particular rose is beautiful." Through disinterest, personal variations of sentiment are eliminated from the aesthetic judgment. That way, the aesthetic judgment of one person will be similar to the aesthetic judgment of another.

This is not, however, the end of the story. Kant begins to explore points of similarity in the make-ups of aesthetic judges. One of these is that all human beings see the world as *formally purposive*. That is, things appear to uniformly work toward some order or end.

When we judge an object aesthetically, our faculties of imagination and understanding engage in what Kant describes as "free play." Free-play judging is judging without bringing the object under any concept. In part, we regard the object as not something we *ought* to understand. We do not consider the object as *one of a certain kind*. We regard the object on its own. For instance, if Sam considers Duchamp's work, *In Advance of a Broken Arm*, as the snow shovel that it perceptually is, then he is not considering it as an aesthetic object. Also, if Sally uses the *Venus di Milo* as a very large doorstop, she is treating it not as an aesthetic object, but as a *tool*. Regarding something as a tool, or under some function it may serve, is not to regard it aesthetically.

In regarding the object under no concept, however, we do not lose sight of its structure and formal purposiveness. To the contrary, to regard an object aesthetically is to see in that object "purposiveness without purpose," as if the object were purposefully designed, but for which no practical use in the ordinary world may be found. The upshot is this: first, we view things as ordered and purposeful; second, we must not consider aesthetic objects as if they were for some specific purpose; and third, we still see the aesthetic object as purposeful—but a "purposeless purposefulness." Confusing? A bit. But this is important in understanding how it is that we regard aesthetic objects similarly, *so* we can make similar aesthetic judgments.

In regarding the object aesthetically, one is able to judge the object in a way such that one's judgment will converge with the judgments of all others evaluating that particular object. When one judges an object to be beautiful, she makes the implicit claim that everyone *ought* to agree with that judgment. She requires from others a judgment similar to hers, else she thinks the other judge is wrong. So, for an object to be a beautiful or aesthetically good object is for it to

(1) be viewed disinterestedly,

(2) be viewed with free play between the imagination and the understanding,

(3) be viewed under no particular category,

(4) be viewed as purposive in design, yet with no actual purpose in the real world, and

(5) be such that if viewed in these ways will produce a favorable judgment, which we expect to be shared by all other properly viewing judges on the basis that everyone has the same cognitive structures for aesthetic judging.

This absence of concepts, this purposiveness-without-purpose, and this free play of the imagination and understanding suggest that there are *no rules* under which we can judge objectively whether an object is beautiful or not. *There is no possibility of creating a formula.* We cannot appeal to a rule to convince our companion that her judgment, different from ours, is incorrect. We must simply appeal to her consideration of the object. We must appeal only to her personal experience of the object, given that she regards the object in the appropriate way: disinterestedly.

No principles of taste can be articulated. When disputes arise, Kant attributes them to a failure on the part of one of the judges: Either she is not judging disinterestedly, she is not exercising a judgment of *taste*—only a judgment of *agreeableness* or *liking*—or she is judging not freely but dependently, that is, she is placing the object under a category of similar objects and judging it against the standard of the set.

Although Kant's aesthetic program solves many of the problems that hurt Hume's account, Kant's program has problems, too. One problem is that the claim that we *would* all judge similarly if in the proper frame of mind is susceptible to empirical scrutiny. We can empirically investigate whether we would all indeed judge alike if we met all of Kant's viewing-conditions. The difficulty lies in the improbability of Kant's being correct empirically in the day-to-day world of aesthetic judging. It would seem that just on the basis of the evidence of common experience that he is mistaken. Take our most aesthetic moments, say when we are at a play or in a gallery. Even then, it is likely that we will find that all of our judgments about what is beautiful and/or what is aesthetically good will not match all of the judgments of another viewer, even if we are both in the same disinterested frame of mind.

Kant may address this criticism as misconceived. It is not a matter, Kant may say, that aesthetic judges, even ones properly disinterested, will actually agree. It is only that in the aesthetic judgment, the judge expects, perhaps demands, that others agree. She is justified in her expectation of agreement. Whether other judges do agree is beside the point.

Another apparent difficulty may be found in examining the Kantian notion of disinterest. By 'disinterested', Kant means that one must attend to the object without any care to its actual existence. One is supposed to pay attention to the object without consideration for anything but the object's appearance, or how she senses the object. However, if we are supposed to pay attention only to the representation, and it is the representation that *solely* contains the value, then it follows that the material object is not what is of value. Possession of an art object, then, is neither important nor encouraged. But this is strange. Surely we are interested in having continued access to the object that gives rise to our aesthetic experience of its contemplative image. Surely we would like to possess aesthetic objects. Moreover, this advice seems to put us in the odd position of believing the image or thought-representation of the object to be more valuable than the original. Take the following example: Suppose that everyone on earth has a clear memory of Monet's *Water Lilies*. Is it the case then that the object itself, which is instrumental only in providing the mental image for us, is no longer valuable? Would we, if the National Gallery were to burn down, not mourn the loss, even if we all perfectly recall the object? This should follow if the object itself is not the point, but only the image is important.

Although Kant has made enormous strides in developing an analysis that accounts for universality of aesthetic judgment while still not offering rules or a formula, his analysis seems to suffer because he does not seem to adequately account for the problem he discussed in connection with Hume: the problem of ultimate and irreconcilable differences between judges.

Again, note that the Kantian analysis of beauty, among all other analyses, stands near the top in terms of its influence and popularity. It is traditionally considered one of the most carefully and well executed examinations of the question in the history of the discipline. Kant stands at an interesting point in the history of philosophy. In all his work, he can be seen as pulling together various strains of philosophy. But even more dramatic is the variety of philosophies that he inspired. One tradition he inspired, though perhaps not immediately or directly, was naturalism.

SECTION FOUR: NATURALISM

As a tradition, naturalism is a rather recent development. 'Naturalism' does not mean a theory of beauty where what is most beautiful is what is most natural, say, in an imitative way. Instead, 'naturalism' is meant in the sense in which the term is used in philosophical circles today. Perhaps the simplest explanation is that naturalism is committed to explaining the world from a scientific perspective, believing that everything that exists can be explained through scientific inquiry. The naturalist attempts to address philosophic questions by appealing to empirical investigation, to scientific method, and to the physical world. So it is that in discussing aesthetics, the naturalist pays a good deal more attention to the empirical inquiries conducted by empirical psychology and other sciences. We will have the opportunity to discuss the relationship between aesthetics and psychology in greater detail later in this section.

GEORGE SANTAYANA

George Santayana's treatment of the question *What is Beauty?* is concise. Santayana suggests that beauty rests entirely on human feelings and human interests. Beauty, says Santayana, is a subjective phenomenon. So this is another theory that takes seriously that "beauty is in the eye of the beholder." As such, we must begin our investigation into beauty with an investigation of what seems to be the essential nature of our psychological states when we are appreciating beauty. Santayana contends that the one element that seems always present is our *attraction* to beauty, and this attraction can be described as a feeling of *pleasure* in regarding beautiful objects. In short, Santayana believes that beauty is *pleasure objectified*, pleasure considered as an aspect or element of the object. For an object to be a beautiful object is for it to

(1) possess pleasure-objectified, such that whenever the object is considered, it will produce a feeling of pleasure in the viewer.

Consider your own experience. When you view an object and have an aesthetic experience, is it not usually pleasurable? While perhaps watching a film like Coppola's *Apocalypse Now* is not pleasurable per se, how can we account for wanting to return to see the film again and again? While pleasure may not be an immediate property of every one of our aesthetic experiences, it certainly seems some part of the equation, else how do we explain our interest in, or our attraction to, aesthetic objects? We are motivated to return to aesthetic situations we have experienced in the past, and we are motivated to seek out new ones. Why is this? Perhaps Santayana is right in saying that pleasure is a necessary ingredient in experiencing aesthetically.

Besides the notion of pleasure objectified, Santayana makes another contribution. His study of beauty occurs not as an historical or didactic exploration. Instead, his method is psychological. He explores what beauty is by addressing what is *felt*—what is *actually* felt—in the presence of beauty. The nature of beauty can then be defined in terms of this essential nature. Aesthetics, for Santayana, is composed of investigation of values that depend directly or indirectly on emotional consciousness, appreciations, preferences, and appetites.

We see in Santayana's analysis a strong anti-Kantian and anti-18th-century bent. We ought *not* be disinterested. Quite the opposite: In order to explore aesthetics, we must acknowledge our vital and deep interests in aesthetic objects. Aesthetic objects are not to be held at arm's length or be divorced from our attachments. They should be considered part of what we indeed are most interested in. It is meaningless to say that what is beautiful to one person *ought* to be beautiful to another. The claim to universality, Santayana tells us, rests on the mistake that beauty is an objective property. Beauty, Santayana argues, is a *subjective* phenomenon.

There are perhaps obvious problems with such an analysis. First, it runs the risk of falling too close to radical subjectivism. Santayana does not seem to provide for similarity of judgment, and without some point of connecting aesthetic judgments about what things are beautiful and what things are aesthetic good, these concepts seem to do little but explain the use of the terms 'beauty' or 'aesthetic goodness' in dictionary form. If all we mean by beauty is some psychological state, then we still must address the question of how aesthetic judgments can actually be correct or incorrect.

Another problem is that there seem to be many items that are pleasurable but not particularly aesthetic. Though one may find great satisfaction and pleasure in cake and ice cream, she would not under normal conditions consider these objects to be aesthetic objects, much less *beautiful* objects.

JOHN DEWEY

John Dewey is the most famous aesthetic naturalist. However, he did not discuss the phenomenon of beauty so much as the *aesthetic experience*. For our purposes, we will focus on what makes an aesthetically good experience.

To begin, we need to be clear on just what Dewey says an aesthetic experience is. Dewey's account of aesthetic experiencing focuses on *experience* as an *interactive* relationship between the perceiver and the object. Dewey uses the term 'experience' in two ways. The first indicates the interactive relationship between the individual and the world around her. The second way indicates a special sort of the first kind. This special sort Dewey calls *an* experience. *An* experience is any experience that principally has the characteristic of being *unified and complete*.

Any experience, regardless of whether it is *an* experience or just a garden-variety experience, is aesthetic to some degree, specifically, to the degree that it incorporates *unity*. But not every experience is as aesthetic as every other experience. Not even every unified experience is as aesthetic as every other, because the degree of unity will vary from experience to experience. Dewey would certainly agree that some event so mundane as brushing one's teeth may not be an aesthetic experience, but it still might have some degree of aesthetic quality.

Those experiences that are truly aesthetic in character are the ones that fit into his classification of *an* experience. While all experiences are aesthetic to the degree that they are unified—which is to say that all experiences are aesthetic to *some* degree—it is the experiences that are *maximally* unified that are truly aesthetic experiences. When a moment is sufficient to itself, is individualized, this is *an* experience. These experiences are typified by viewing paintings, listening to symphonies, reading novels, and so forth.

This of course puts the onus for the aesthetic quality of the object or event on the subject and her experience. The judgment of whether an experience is *an* experience is made solely on the basis of the felt experience of the individual perceiver. Only in her experience can the object in question be judged to be aesthetic, and it follows that the aesthetic quality of the experience then is something that is personal. On the face of things, this makes for a subjectivistic account of aesthetic judgment. We must be careful, however, not to allow comparability of judgments to be sacrificed due to subjectivity. Dewey avoids this danger.

In gaining insight into an aesthetic object, a person is able to appreciate the aesthetic properties, understand and appreciate their relation to one another, and then understand and appreciate the relation of the work to herself as subject and the relation the object bears to others of its kind and its environment. In working through all of this, the subject comes to have an experience that is not merely momentarily pleasurable or even aesthetic. She comes to build a structure that will allow for more frequent and greater appreciation of this object, of objects of its kind, and, consequently, of aesthetic objects in general.

The individual experience is what is at the heart of aesthetic judgment. However, it follows from this account that the great works of art, or, we might say, the most enduring aesthetic objects, are those that provide the richest aesthetic experience or create most frequently *an* experience. In this way, the autonomy of the individual can coexist with the regularity that we perceive in the history of art and in the consensus about what sorts of things make for good aesthetic objects (sunsets, flowers, and whales' sounds) and what sorts of things generally do not (dirty dishes and coughing).

In formulating his view, Dewey is careful to focus on the experience of the *common person*. Careful not to dictate which experiences are aesthetic and which are not, Dewey instead allows for the decision of the common person. Dewey's interest is in the ordinary. If he can capture what occurs in the ordinary experience of aesthetic qualities, then he will have formulated a theory that takes the empirical description of what occurs as basic. In this regard, Dewey's program is similar to Santayana's. As we saw with Santayana, when the common experience of humans is taken as basic, the focus is not on the divorce from interest in the objects believed to be aesthetic. Quite the reverse. Dewey shows a common person who is vitally interested in the objects that she experiences aesthetically, and the interest and attention that she invests the objects with are just those characteristics that lead her to experience the object aesthetically. The experience is aesthetic because it captures her attention and interest so vividly. She is enraptured with the experience.

Now, it must be granted that the disinterest that Kant had in mind is not exactly the same sort of disinterest that Dewey rejects. Kant maintains that one must be disinterested *but still* attentive and empathetic toward the object. The idea of attention and empathy may be more in line with what Dewey advocates. In any case, Dewey's commitment to the common person's experience allows the aesthetic experience to be characterized by a much wider ranger of emotions and mental states than the disinterest approach. This makes Dewey's job—or the job of any naturalistic aesthetician—the discovery of what constitutes aesthetic experience for the ordinary person, that is, to find the patterns in the aesthetic experiencing of common people.

For an object to be an aesthetically good object is for it to

(1) be capable of creating *an* experience in viewers, based on the *unity* of the experience, and

(2) be able to do so on a regular and systematic basis.

Dewey has not enjoyed in current times the kind of examination that other historically influential aestheticians have. However, there is a question concerning whether events that are highly unified, yet thought to be quite unaesthetic, present a reason to suspect Dewey's account. The complaint is that we seem to find a counterexample to Dewey's analysis in the experience of works of art that *specifically* incorporate a lack of unity.

Another criticism of Dewey's account is that in the ordinary world, when we do feel the sense of unity, sometimes this is definitely *not* aesthetic in character: say, unpleasant experiences such as riding on a very crowded subway, experiences that are highly unified but that we would not ordinarily describe as being aesthetic in any way.

Aesthetics is a much broader field for Dewey than it is for most other aestheticians. For him, hard lines between aesthetic and nonaesthetic experience, as traditionally viewed, are blurred. In dissolving boundaries, Dewey lets in much that other aestheticians seek to keep out. But this is no criticism of his program. Indeed, for a life that is *more aesthetic* than less, we should be grateful to Dewey and his account.

NATURALISM CONSIDERED

How relevant is psychology to aesthetics? Generally speaking, there are three major problems with the use of psychology in philosophy. First, some questions posed in philosophy seem too big to be answered by psychology. It would be a mistake to ask psychology to answer questions that are essentially broader than psychology is supposed to be able to answer. *What is Art?* is a question ill suited to being answered by psychology. Psychology does not pretend to have answers to questions like this. However, there is a large set of philosophical questions that psychology *is* prepared to answer, or at least shed light on. We have seen psychology's use in the views of Santayana, Dewey, and a bit with Beardsley.

The second problem is commonly referred to as the *naturalistic fallacy*, which some explain as attempting to derive an *ought* from an *is*, attempting to derive the *prescriptive* from the *descriptive*. That is, the attempt to determine the nature of values on the basis of facts. Some naturalists, though, do not use psychology to explore what *ought to be* valuable, but to study what already *is* taken to be valuable. Psychology does not tell us that it is (say) aesthetic experience that is *valuable*—though it can tell us that aesthetic experience is *valued*. What psychology does do is to provide a means for exploration *once the philosophical work is completed*. If this is taken as the model of how psychology *is* used, then the question of the so-called naturalistic fallacy is not one we need even concern ourselves with.

The third problem for the use of psychology in aesthetics is rather obvious: Science does not tell one what aesthetic experience is unless one can already recognize instances. This is how it is with all psychological scientific studies: The testimony of the individual, or the behavior of the individual, must first be identified before anything theoretical can be constructed. The conclusion is that we can, once the initial philosophical analysis is provided, use psychology to help us settle aesthetic issues.

The debate is not settled. However, many debates in aesthetics are unsettled, and none of the difficulty ought to prompt us to dismiss a theory too early. Aesthetic naturalism has not been explored as thoroughly as other traditions. If some of the reasons for this are those mentioned just above, it would be good to dispel some of the myths.

CHAPTER 9

Reviewing Art and Art Criticism

Suppose you and a friend decide to go to the movies. You pull out the newspapers to find out what is playing. You and your friend each take half of the movie section, and each of you takes turns suggesting possibilities. But every time you suggest a film, your friend replies by saying how much the critics disliked it. Your reply is that you have frequently found that the critics do not know what they are talking about. And who are they, anyway, telling you what you should and should not see?

This is, in part, exactly the problem we will discuss here. While we tend to foster some animosity toward critics who persistently disagree with our "novice" opinions, we nonetheless continue to read or listen to what they have to say. Why is this? What special abilities does the film critic have that ordinary moviegoers do not have?

Criticism is the formal treatment of educated viewing. Indeed, criticism might be, in its broadest usage, synonymous with educated viewing. Part of our present task is to determine just what is meant by 'criticism'. Many believe that to *criticize* is to *devalue* an object. If one criticizes his mother-in-law's cooking, the intent is to say that it ranks low on the scale of edibility, that it is not tasty. Indeed, 'criticize' is commonly used in this way. And this is a perfectly fine use of the word when we are discussing aesthetic objects. However, it is not the whole story.

When the word 'criticize' is used in aesthetics, we do not mean *just* detraction from value. When we watch film critics such as Roger Ebert on television—a good example of popular art criticism—we fully expect that he will berate some films but also that he will praise others. Thumbs-down works only when there is the option of thumbs-up. So art criticism need not be merely negative, just as *critical thinking* need not merely describe a negative activity.

Critical thinking—or critical reasoning—shares a great deal in common with art criticism. In both, we seek to justify our beliefs. We are interested in avoiding reasoning errors in the construction of our arguments or belief-defenses, and we are interested in providing evidence for our claims that will ideally convince our opponent that we are right. The evaluative aspect of art criticism does exactly this. It focuses on justifying our claims that a work of art is beautiful, aesthetically good, ugly, or aesthetically bad. We cite evidence—which usually takes the form of drawing attention to various aspects of the aesthetic object under consideration—to demonstrate the reasonableness of our views. Moreover, we cite evidence to tangibly demonstrate that we recommend those views to the person to whom we are giving this evidence.

THE CRITICAL REVIEW

There are four components in an ideal critical art review:

(1) Description
(2) Information
(3) Interpretation
(4) Evaluation

While certainly not every critical art review will have all of these four components, it is likely that the longer reviews—such as are found in magazines like the *New Yorker*—will address each of these. Art reviews that are found in books will tend to go heavier on information and interpretation. Art reviews found in newspapers will tend toward just description and evaluation. But the ideal critical art review can be understood most easily as having all four parts.

The first step in any reputable critical review is description. To describe an aesthetic object (or event) is perhaps the most basic form of aesthetic review. When we describe an object, we mean to pick out features of that object that anyone with working senses who is paying close attention would also pick out. We mean to be offering a purely objective account of what is physically present before us, and so we mean as much as possible to keep out any editorializing or evaluative commentary. If we embellish our description by sneaking into it evaluative comments, then we rob from our description any work it will do for us in evidencing claims. Unless two people who disagree over the aesthetic merits of an object can agree on what is objectively present before them, there is no way that either one of them can cite objective, base properties as evidence for her claim that the work has certain (middle-level and higher-level) aesthetic features. So it is important to keep description as value-free as possible. The art critic who indulges in providing his evaluative comments along with his description of the object he is reviewing reduces the value and power of his review substantially.

Now, is it really the case that description can be purely value-free? This is unclear. Fundamentally, the choice of describing certain features and ignoring others involves evaluative decisions on the part of the critic. The choice of what elements to relate to audiences as important is itself a matter of judgment. If a critic talks about the flowing character of the garments of the Virgin Mary, she tends to single this out as somehow important to the sculpture. Furthermore, if we believe that description can include mention of middle-level aesthetic properties (this is discussed in chapter 1), and we further believe that these properties cannot be identified without appealing to the critic's taste, her aesthetic sensibilities, then description of this sort will clearly not be value-free. Description, while it is not supposed to be value-laden, nonetheless can be associated with evaluatory processes. But the upshot is that description, though perhaps a bit value-laden, is the least "critical" facet of criticism. At base, a description of an object is supposed to be a value-free account of what the viewer senses in attending closely to the object as an object.

Now, one last point: Description *is not* interpretation. Interpretation deals with meanings, intentions, expressions, and the like. Description, on the other hand, deals solely or primarily with the sensory embodiment itself. One could, in describing the *Pietà*, say that it is a huge chunk of marble, fashioned in a large pyramidal-triangular shape, depicting (at least on the front face of the marble) a youngish woman, with heavy flowing garments, cradling the limp dead body of a young, thin, unadorned man. Taking a further step, one could suggest that the young woman is the Virgin Mary (at a younger age than she would have been at the point of the Crucifixion), and the young man Jesus, just after the Crucifixion. Either or both of these are descriptions of the sculpture. And one could, in giving a description of the sculpture, become a great deal more detailed or even more general.

The second part of an ideal critical art review is information. This is the part of the critical process where the reviewer offers information designed to give viewers a better understanding of the object *as* an aesthetic object. Ultimately, this information is meant to increase appreciation or enrich experience of the object. The information the critic might offer may include the following:

(A) What are the origins of the work? Who was the artist, and what were her circumstances?

(B) What was the environment in which the work was created? When was it created? Where?

(C) What was the context of the work? What was the society in which it was created like? What were the religious, moral, and social values of that time and place?

(D) What was the genre of the work? How does it relate/compare to other of its kind? What *is* its kind?

(E) What is the history of the work? Was it valued when it was first created? Who valued it? How did it come to be in this museum/gallery/collection?

(F) (And for natural objects…) How did this object come to exist? Who found it, or who *adopted* it as art?

These are just some of the kinds of questions that the critic might address in giving information about an aesthetic object. There are, no doubt, many other questions that might be relevant to a review of the object.

The third part of an ideal critical art review is interpretation. Interpretation and exploration of the meaning of a work of art is an important part of reviewing an aesthetic object. We discussed interpretation in detail in chapter 6, so we will not say more here.

EVALUATION

Evaluation, the fourth part of an ideal critical art review, is perhaps the most important part of art criticism. This aspect of criticism is included in more reviews than any other aspect. Earlier, we reviewed several positions about what makes a thing beautiful or aesthetically good, and/or what makes for our *knowing* that something is beautiful or aesthetically good. The most useful, for criticism, are the following:

I.   Aristotle: for an object to be *good* is for that object to

   (1)   be an object that functions highly as an instance of the kind under which it is being considered.

   However, for an object to be beautiful, or aesthetically good, is for that object to

    (1)   be ordered,

    (2)   be symmetrical,

    (3)   be definite, and

    (4)   meet each of these criteria to a high degree.

II.   Shaftesbury: for an object to be beautiful is for that object to

   (1)   be considered from a disinterested attitude, and

   (2)   participate in the essence of beauty, which is identified with possessing the formal quality of unity-in-multiplicity.

III.   Hutcheson: for an object to be beautiful is for that object to

   (1)   be considered from a disinterested attitude, and

   (2)   possess the formal quality of uniformity-amongst-variety.

IV.   Beardsley: for an object to be aesthetically good is for it to

   (1)   be unified, and/or intense, and/or complex, and

     (2)   be such that it prompts in attentive perceivers a pleasurable experience characterized by unity, and/or intensity, and/or complexity.

V.   Dewey: for an object to be an aesthetically good object is for it to

     (1)   be capable of creating *an* experience in viewers, primarily based on the *unity* of the experience, and

     (2)   be able to do so on a regular and systematic basis.

VI.   Hume (true judge): for an object to be a beautiful and/or aesthetically good object is for it to

     (1)   provoke aesthetic sentiment in appropriately disposed competent critics, *true judges*.

VII.   Kant (universality): for an object to be a beautiful and/or aesthetically good object is for it to

     (1)   be viewed disinterestedly,

     (2)   be viewed with free play between the imagination and the understanding,

     (3)   be viewed under no particular category,

     (4)   be viewed as purposive in design, yet with no actual purpose in the real world, and

     (5)   be such that if viewed in these ways will produce a favorable judgment, which we expect to be shared by all other properly viewing judges on the basis that everyone has the same cognitive structures for aesthetic judging.

Aristotle's use of the term 'good' is a marvelous base upon which the critic or educated viewer might build. If Sam wishes to rate a ballet, he may first consider the dance *as* ballet. That is, he will consider whether the dance functioned highly as an instance of the kind *ballet*. Were the moves executed well against the standard of the way ballet moves are generally executed? If the ballerina executed a plié, was it a good plié—that is, as pliés go, did it do everything that pliés are supposed to do, and do it effectively, flowingly, softly, and so forth?

Of course, this criterion only works if there is a standard. Many times there is a standard available, but what if someone asks, "Yes, I realize that it was a good ballet, but was it beautiful or good art?" Were Sam a critic, he may have been more uncomfortable with the response that Aristotle would have given. That is, while he might have found the performance highly ordered, symmetrical, and definite, he may still not have found the performance to be particularly good, or vice versa. The accounts of Shaftesbury and Hutcheson, where the criteria are spelled out quite precisely, suffer from the same problem: Sam may find the criterion fulfilled yet not find the performance beautiful or good, or he might find the performance beautiful/good but not find that it fulfilled one or the other of the criteria. In any event, Aristotle's functionary account of goodness, where we measure goodness against a standard, is still one of the best tools of a critic or educated viewer.

Beardsley, though he offers a sort of formula, is more successful than Shaftesbury or Hutcheson. This is for several reasons. First, Beardsley does not look for one characteristic, which if present makes for beauty or goodness. Instead, he gives us categories: unity, intensity, and complexity. Through a consideration of the work in these categories, we are able to access the beauty or goodness of the work. Not every work that is highly unified, intense, and complex will be beautiful/good. But all good works, Beardsley suggests, rank high on the scale of at least one of these criteria. One thing that Beardsley offers is a focus on the *experience* of the viewer. Instead of focusing in a straightforward way on the object itself and alone, Beardsley seeks to base the value of the art on the experience of the viewer. That experience, as we have discussed, is intimately tied to the object of attention. But that does not negate the importance of Beardsley's suggestion that what is aesthetically valuable is, at some stage or to some degree, valuable because of the viewer's experience. Beardsley's evaluative system is derived in part from John Dewey's. Dewey, you will recall, says that what is important is the experience of the individual. If that experience contains a high degree of unity, then that experience is an aesthetic one. And, it would seem to follow, the higher the unity, the better the aesthetic experience.

Citation of her experience is another good tool for the critic or educated viewer. If one is allowed to write in her appraisal how she felt or how she was moved, she is able to more eloquently and precisely advise readers of the value of the work. If one is limited to a discussion only of the properties of the work, suggesting that this plié or that was good, she is not as convincing in her recommendation of the work.

EMOTIVISM

This brings us to an important point. Some philosophers believe that the judgments we make about works of art are *not* really about whether the object is *really* beautiful or *really* aesthetically good. Some believe that the judgments are merely expressions *of our own feelings*. In making aesthetic judgments, they say, we are merely *expressing our feelings* about how we felt in viewing or hearing the work. The judgment, "Monet's *Water Lilies* is a beautiful and aesthetically good work of art," translates for members of this camp into "*Water Lilies*, yea! Hurray for *Water Lilies!*"

This is *emotivism*. Emotivists believe that when we express judgments about goodness and badness, beauty and ugliness, we are merely *emoting*, that is, expressing our emotions with regard to how we feel in attention to whatever work we mean to be evaluating. There is nothing cognitive in our judgment, they say; we are merely expressing our *sentiments* about the work.

Emotivism is not, it may be important to note, a theory about the existence of aesthetic properties or the correctness of aesthetic claims. Emotivism is a theory about the *meanings* of aesthetic terms. The emotivist holds that aesthetic judgments mean nothing other than expressions of emotion.

There are problems with such a view. The most central is that this makes the role of the critic—or even the educated viewer—substantially less than it is in a nonemotivist (perhaps realist) framework. If the critic is *merely* expressing how she felt in attendance to the object, then why should one listen to her? Why not simply go, look at the object, and then feel the way that one will feel, and let that be the end of it? Perhaps, one might answer, we use the critic as a sort of *scout*. The critic scouts around the art exhibits and performances, and then gives us her emotive reactions so we can make a more informed decision about whether we want to take the time and trouble to go to the exhibit or performance. Or perhaps the critic's role is only supposed to be that of *reviewer*. She offers lots of information and perhaps offers her emotive reactions, but this is all. But in the final analysis, this leaves the role of the critic substantially deflated.

HUME'S EVALUATIVE TECHNIQUES

David Hume tries to answer this problem. Hume believed that certain forms or qualities are designed to please viewers, and other forms and qualities, as a matter of fact displease. Moreover, these forms and qualities are *objective*. They exist as part of objects in the world, quite apart from the emotional states of viewing individuals. If Hume is correct, then emotivism does not capture what we really mean when we say that a thing is beautiful. If Hume is correct, our aesthetic judgments are matters of rightness and wrongness. And indeed, many objects are nearly universally considered beautiful. When one sees a sunset off the Gulf Coast of Florida that has many colors, each deep and vibrant, she may fully expect that everyone on earth who would see this sunset would be as eager as she to declare it beautiful. And this is because, Hume says, the properties of that sunset are indeed beautiful.

So if one rejects emotivism on the grounds that there is no way to account for the vast similarity of taste regarding certain objects, like the sunset, then the emotivist position does not seem as tenable as it once might have. The emotivist cannot explain similarity between judgments *at all*. For the emotivist, similar judgments are merely coincidences. Furthermore, any *consistency* we would find, *even among our own judgments*, would be a matter of coincidence. This seems rather odd. One can predict a close friend's taste in art and usually be right. Surely there is a pattern to one's likes and dislikes, and this pattern is fairly stable. The pattern is due to consistency among an individual's aesthetic judgments. Furthermore, if the prediction fails in one situation, we can appeal to the properties of the object to establish whether one just failed to see where this instance was really not a part of the pattern, or whether she missed something and is willing to revise her original judgment. But the emotivist cannot explain any of this: It is merely a matter of coincidence.

The problem now is to try to answer, perhaps from the Humean perspective, how it is that we have so much *diversity* among our aesthetic judgments. After all, widespread disagreement is obvious fuel for the emotivist position. If there are certain forms and qualities that objectively please, thought Hume, then there must lie behind these forms and qualities certain *principles* of beauty and aesthetic goodness. This was the road traveled by Shaftesbury and Hutcheson. Unfortunately, the principles they advocate may be too strict. But principles that are too loose will be equally worthless.

Hume attempts to solve this problem by focusing on the judge or evaluator herself. Diversity among judgments, Hume conjectured, is a problem of the judge, not of the object. It is not as though the object changes when being viewed by different individuals. The change must be in the difference between individuals. If there are individuals who are insensitive to art, ignorant about art, inattentive to the artwork, or immature in their exposure to artworks, then it stands to reason that their judgments may be flawed. Hume suggests that we need to draw up what would go into making someone a good judge. Good judges, then, would be able to determine whether some individual object does have forms and qualities that do indeed please, that are beautiful or aesthetically good. Hume's ideal critic, his *true judge*, has the following traits:

(A) She has a serenity of mind (this is mentioned earlier than the other five),

(B) she has a delicacy of taste,

(C) she is well practiced,

(D) she is versed in comparison between objects,

(E) she is free from prejudice, and

(F) she has good sense, or her senses work very well.

As we saw before, the *true judge* account is not free from difficulty. Is it possible to find such a *true judge*? Does the list of traits that we include in our *true judge* merely reflect our own values, interests, and prejudices? And what if it happened that if we found two *true judges* and they disagreed—irreconcilably and incompatibly—about some work? While the theory might have some bugs, it does give the critic good instruction. A good critic, we might agree, has to some degree the traits that Hume would include in his *true judge*. A good critic is sensitive, able to concentrate, well versed in criticism and in the sorts of things he is criticizing, impartial, and keen.

KANT'S EVALUATIVE TECHNIQUES

Kant begins from the work of Shaftesbury/Hutcheson and the work of Hume. How can we account for similarity and diversity of judgment? The key, Kant thought, is twofold:

(1) Each person has a similar "common sense" and similar cognitive structures for understanding the world. We are all built relevantly alike, and so the mechanisms we use to make judgments are similar.

(2) Our judgments are *not* merely sentimental or emotional. Aesthetic judgments are partly *cognitive* judgments. They involve what Kant calls a free play between the understanding and the imagination.

But, of course, the aesthetic judgment still involves likes and dislikes, and so it is not on completely firm ground. Since one's likes and dislikes are bound to be different from another's, they will interfere with convergence of our individual aesthetic judgments. Kant answers this problem in suggesting that in order to be properly disposed to being a good judge, one must be *disinterested* in her evaluations. Given disinterest on the part of the judge, and given that we all have similar faculties for understanding the world, we would all judge similarly. (The biggest problem is that the claim that we would all judge alike is open to empirical scrutiny. If we have two judges, alike in attentiveness and alike in disinterest, would they always judge similarly?)

Even in this brief review we see the benefit of the Kantian program for the critic or educated viewer. Though we may not be able to adopt the Kantian program as the correct one for any evaluatory procedures of any critic, Kant does spotlight the importance of disinterest. On a straightforward reading, he is casting light on the necessity of impartiality in judging, and this is no doubt very important for the good critic.

ART CRITICISM CONSIDERED

There may be good reason to believe that the critic offers *real* judgments about the object, and by 'real' is meant that the judgments of the critic, properly disposed and outfitted, are really true or false. This is the subject of "aesthetic realism," and there are in the literature just about as many arguments against it as in favor of it. Is it possible to construct aesthetic judgments that refer to facts about the world? This is not an argument we can take up here, in this overview of the history of aesthetics, but it is crucial to understanding aesthetics with any serious depth. And it is crucial in terms of deciding whether the art critic is a person whose judgments are worth listening to.

If the art critic offers to her readers something of value, then probably what she offers will enhance his experience of aesthetic or art objects. In the offering of information that is purely descriptive, contextual, interpretative, and evaluative, the critic provides a means through which the educated viewer may enliven and enrich his aesthetic experiences. So it follows that the role of the critic is to provide her readers with appropriate information about works of art. And it follows from our discussion that there are many characteristics that go into making a good critic. From our previous discussions, we find the following characteristics of a good critic:

(1) The critic should know the various genre of art that she criticizes, so that she can make comparisons with standards of those genre (Aristotle, Hume).

(2) The critic should be objective, impartial, and disinterested (Shaftesbury, Hutcheson, Hume, Kant).

(3) The critic should be sensitive and introspective to her own appreciation/experience of the work (Hume, Kant). Her reactions provide (i) a more eloquent account of her judgment of the work and (ii) a basis for comparison with the reactions of her readers.

(4) The critic should have a delicacy of taste (Hume).

(5) The critic should have a serenity of mind (Hume), be able to focus, be able to concentrate, and be highly attentive.

(6) The critic should be well practiced (Hume); she should know her subject.

(7) The critic should have keen senses (Hume).

(8) The critic should be able to pick out what she values in her experience of the work (Dewey, Beardsley). She may value order (Aristotle, Kant), symmetry (Aristotle), definiteness (Aristotle, Kant), unity (Dewey, Beardsley), intensity (Beardsley), complexity (Beardsley), unity-in-multiplicity (Shaftesbury), uniformity-amongst-variety (Hutcheson), or any other of the myriad properties of the work, or her experience of the work, that contribute to the aesthetic value of the work.

(9) The critic should be equally clear about what it is that she believes *harms* the value of the work.

Items (8) and (9) amount to saying that the critic ought to provide *reasons* in support of her judgment. The critic's job, many would assert, is to offer *reasons for her likes and dislikes*. This is a popular conception of the role of the critic. And it is something that takes training and practice.

This may take us back into a discussion of what role sentiment and what role cognition play in the formation of an aesthetic judgment. But (1) if the judgment is cognitive to any degree, there will be reasons that the critic can offer, and (2) reasons need not merely issue forth from a cognitive base: Perhaps a reason for disliking a certain work is that it made the critic feel distinctly uncomfortable. While we might want additional information, we can still accept this simple report of emotion as a *reason* that the critic's judgment was as it was—or at least accept it as a *cause* of the critic's judgment.

The critic who has all of the traits mentioned above might be quite rare, but these are the traits that many aestheticians have identified as important to accurate aesthetic appraisals. The critic has a vital role to play with regard to art. Her presence cannot be dismissed, and if she is properly disposed and outfitted, then what she has to say with regard to the artworks may well be worth listening to.

Appendix: An Outline of the History of Western Aesthetics

I. REPRESENTATION / MIMESIS

   A. Introduction

      (1) For an object to be an art object is for it to

         (a) be an artifact, and

         (b) be an imitation of some object—presumably natural—in the world.

      (2) The degree to which the imitation resembles the natural object is the measure of how good the work is. This theory makes imitation or representation not only the criterion of an artwork but also the criterion for judging value.

   B. **Plato** (428–347 B.C.)

      (1) For an object to be an art object is for it to

         (a) be an artifact, and

         (b) be an imitation of some object in the world.
Any work, then, created either with the intention of being viewed as a representation of something in the world, or actually being viewed that way, is an art object.

      (2) Imitation is not good. The picture of a bed is three steps from reality. It is a picture (not able to be slept on) of a bed (a particular physical or "contingent" bed) that issues from the Form of "bedness" (which is the true reality).

      (3) Reasons for censoring art:

         (a) Art is an imitation of an imitation.

> (b)   Art is physical and detracts from true Beauty, which exists in the Heaven of Ideas.
>
> (c)   One cannot learn from art, since it is far from the truth.

(4)   Art has value *only* in support of the state. Art should celebrate only the virtues of the heroes and gods. It should not show weaknesses. Tragedy, in raising emotion, harms the character of the viewer.

C. **Aristotle** (384–322 B.C.)

(1)   For an object to be an art object is for it to

> (a)   be an artifact,
>
> (b)   be an imitation of *the universal* in nature, and
>
> (c)   be delightful to viewers (hearers and so forth).

(2)   Imitation is natural to animals, particularly man. Art is founded on two things:

> (a)   imitation is a natural part of animals' behavior, and
>
> (b)   it is natural to delight in works of imitation.

(3)   The artist looks to the universal or archetype, not to the specific. Art is imitation, but the imitations are better than the originals in nature. The artist expresses the universal element in things.

(4)   For any object to be good, it must be an object that functions highly as an instance of the kind under which it is being considered.

(5)   For an object to be beautiful (or aesthetically good) is for that object to

> (a)   be ordered,
>
> (b)   be symmetrical,
>
> (c)   be definite, and
>
> (d)   meet each of these criteria to a high degree.
> Beauty is a property of the structure of objects. Beauty is matter of size and order. Beautiful objects exhibit *closure* or have definite limits.

(6)   Catharsis is the purging, purifying, or exorcising of tragic emotions through attention to some art object that exhibits and arouses emotion.

(7)   The Elements of Tragedy are spectacle, melody, diction, thought, character, and fable/plot. A tragedy should portray a balanced person passing through misfortune brought about by some error of judgment and not by vice or depravity.

D. The Medievals

(1)   **St. Augustine** (354–430)
For an object to be beautiful is for it to exhibit unity, number, equality, proportion and order. Unity is the most basic notion.

(2)   **St. Thomas Aquinas** (1224–1274)
Beauty depends on the form. Beauty includes three conditions:

(a)   integrity or perfection,

(b)   due proportion or harmony, and

(c)   brightness or clarity (as light is a symbol of divine beauty and truth).

E.   Problems with a Representational Theory of Art

(1)   Not all art is representational. Much of art, especially in the 20th century, is abstract or formalistic. Also, much music is not representational.

(2)   An object might well represent in more than one way or represent different things to different viewers. For the Representational Theory to work, does the viewer have to see the object represented the same way the artist did? Or the same way that all other viewers do?

II.   BRITISH EMPIRICISM

A.   Introduction

(1)   The British Empiricists were interested not primarily in what constitutes a work of art. Instead, they were interested in how we evaluate art and other aesthetic objects. How do we tell if something is beautiful or aesthetically good? What is the faculty of *taste?*

B.   **Lord Shaftesbury** (Anthony Ashley Cooper, the third earl of Shaftesbury; 1671–1713)

(1)   Shaftesbury was a Platonist. He believed that the real property of beauty exists apart from beautiful (physical) objects. It exists in a spiritual realm.

(2)   Shaftesbury was the first aesthetician who used the concept of "disinterest." A viewer, in order to properly judge an object aesthetically, must be disinterested; she must have no self-interest in the object, particularly in the possession of the object.

(3)   We all have something which he called "Moral Sense," an inward eye that grasps beauty and does so immediately. This Moral Sense is, in part, the faculty of *taste.*

(4)   If an object is beautiful, then it must and does possess unity-in-multiplicity. For an object to be beautiful is for that object to

(a)   be considered from a disinterested attitude, and

(b)   participate in beauty, which is identified with possession of the formal property of unity-in-multiplicity.

C.   **Francis Hutcheson** (1694–1746)

(1)   Hutcheson was an empiricist and a relational realist. Unlike Shaftesbury, he believed that beauty is found through the agent's attention to the object's properties.

(2)   We all have an "Internal Sense." This is our power of perceiving the Beauty of regularity, order, and harmony. Experience shows that there is a great agreement among individuals as to their perceptual likes and dislikes. The Internal Sense is Hutcheson's faculty

of taste. It was, for Hutcheson, as real and present as any other faculty, though one can not physically locate any "taste-organ" as one could locate the eyes or ears.

(3)   The greater the capacity of our Internal Sense, the more of a "genius of taste" we have. This capacity grows through practice and increased sensitivity.

(4)   Our Internal Senses are stimulated when we observe *uniformity-amongst-variety* in objects.

(5)   One must, as with Shaftesbury, be in the attitude of disinterest in order to properly judge.

(6)   For an object to be beautiful is for that object to

    (a)   be considered from a disinterested attitude, and

    (b)   possess the formal property of uniformity-amongst-variety.

D. **Joseph Addison** (1672–1719)

(1)   Addison reacted to Hutcheson's claim that there was any such thing as a special faculty that accounted for the universality of taste. He based his theory of taste on what science, what psychology, would have said was there. Hutcheson's "faculty" might simply be an *ability* to discern and appreciate or enjoy beauty.

(2)   Three qualities, when in the object, give rise in the spectator to a favorable aesthetic judgment:

    (a)   greatness or sublimity,

    (b)   uncommonness or novelty, and/or

    (c)   beauty.

(3)   Addison offers two tests for determining the correctness of our aesthetic judgment:

    (a)   the test of time, and

    (b)   that one is pleased with the *proper* qualities of what one is perceiving.

(4)   We can know that we are pleased with the "proper" qualities of the object when we are *disinterested.*

E. **Archibald Alison** (1757–1839)

(1)   Alison thought that it was imagination, or certain associations, that made for aesthetic experiencing. The spectator exercises her mind, her *attentive* contemplation, in order to more fully experience the nature of the object, and in so doing experience the object as fully aesthetically as she can. Without this mindful/imaginative activity, the experience is not aesthetic but one of mere pleasure.

(2)   In spite of his use of the notion of "associations," he stressed the importance of disinterest in aesthetic contemplation. If we are encumbered by personal or practical interests, this will interfere

with the depth to which we can contemplatively attend to the object, and with our experience of beauty.

F. **David Hume** (1711–1776)

(1) Hume's starting point is the notion of *De gustibus non disputandum est*: There is no disputing tastes or preferences. There are great inconsistencies in the individual tastes.

(2) Hume's Paradox of Taste: If we just judge the way we wish—on our feeling and opinions—how is it that we can assess that some of the judgments are wrong?

Hume says that all sentiment is right, because sentiment refers to nothing beyond itself and it is always real, whenever a man is conscious of it. But all judgments of the understanding are not right, because they refer to something beyond themselves, to real matters of fact.

(3) Hume says it appears that "amidst all the variety and caprice of tastes, there are certain general principles of approbation and blame, whose influence a careful eye may trace in all operations of the mind. Some particular forms or qualities…are calculated to please, and others displease." There are objective properties that regularly please, and others that regularly displease.

However, "these rules of judgment are not fixed a priori. As with practical sciences, the laws come through experience. But though all the general rules of art are founded only on experience and on the *observation of the common sentiments of human nature*, we must not imagine that on every occasion the feelings of men will be conformable to these rules.

"Every work of art has also a certain end or purpose, for which it is calculated; and is to be deemed more or less perfect as it is more or less fitted to attain this end. These ends we must carry constantly in our view, when we pursue any performance; and we must be able to judge how far the means employed are adapted to their respective purposes."

(4) An object is beautiful only if it provokes aesthetic sentiment in appropriately disposed competent critics, in *true judges*.

(5) *True judges* have the following traits:

(a) serenity of mind (mentioned earlier than the other five),

(b) delicacy of taste,

(c) they are well practiced,

(d) they are versed in comparison between objects,

(e) they are free from prejudice, and

(f) they have good sense (or their senses work very well).
Thus, though the principles of taste are universal, and nearly, if not entirely the same in all people—yet few are qualified to give judgment on any work of art or establish their own sentiment as the standard of beauty.

    (6) Problems

        (a) In order for Hume to be correct, it ought to be the case that in all of aesthetic study, a set of principles that confer aesthetic merit ought to have been drawn up. That is, if we can find patterns among judgments, we ought to be able to identify the objective properties that give rise to these judgments. Possible answer: There is a logical possibility of such a list, but the probability of actually identifying it is very low, given the extremely large amount of data that must be accounted for.

        (b) We tend, in the description of our *true judge*, to build in just those attributes that we ourselves believe would contribute to his ability to judge correctly. We tend to make our *true judge* in our own image.

        (c) Finally, what about the possibility of irreconcilable and incompatible differences between *true judges*? Suppose that two persons, each equally and well qualified to be *true judges* and each appropriately disposed, were to judge an object, and their judgments differ in a manner where reconciliation is impossible and consistency is violated.

G. **Henry Home** (Lord Kames; 1696–1782)

    (1) The fundamental principles of the fine arts must be drawn from human nature. The general rule for the occurrence of emotions is that we love what is agreeable, and every work of art that is conformable to the natural course of our ideas is so far agreeable.

    (2) Aesthetic qualities are of two sorts: those that an object possesses in itself and those that it has in relation to other objects. Qualities of the first sort are grandeur, sublimity, motion, force, novelty, laughableness, and beauty. The relational qualities are resemblance, dissimilitude, uniformity, and variety.

H. **Edmund Burke** (1729–1797)

    (1) *On the Sublime and the Beautiful* marked the point at which aesthetic taste in England changed from classical formalism to romanticism.

    (2) His task was to determine what qualities bring out in us the notion of beauty (love without desire) and sublimity (astonishment without actual danger). After analyzing the concepts, he said that Beauty is what "relaxes the solids of the whole system." Burke, the strictest empiricist, offers a sort of *physiological* aesthetics.

III. UNIVERSALITY / KANTIAN AESTHETICS

A. Introduction

    (1) Kantian aesthetics, like much of Kant's work, is not easily categorized along the work of others. Kant thought in revolutionary ways. He did not engage in "speculative metaphysics," however, but sought to describe our experience of the world and the structure of that experience—a structure common to us all.

(2) Kant's work follows shortly after **Alexander Baumgarten** (1714–1762) coined the word 'aesthetics' in 1735. Baumgarten made a systematic attempt at a metaphysics of art. He introduced 'aesthetic' to designate the section of *empirical psychology* that treats the faculty of sensible knowledge.

B. **Immanuel Kant** (1724–1804)

   (1) Background

   (a) Kant rejects the attempts of Shaftesbury and Hutcheson to make aesthetic judgments matters of feeling. But he also rejects Baumgarten's attempts to treat the concept of the beautiful as a science. Hume's treatment of the paradox of taste was an influence on Kant's work.

   (b) In the *Critique of Judgment*, Kant begins by saying that nature is "formally purposive." Nature seems to work together *as if* it were designed purposively. This principle is not objective, but a *subjective maxim of judgment*. We necessarily assume and expect that nature will display unity-in-diversity, or this working together.

   (2) The Claim to Universality

   (a) Aesthetic judgments claim universality. When we say that something is beautiful, we fully expect that *everyone* will agree with us in our judgment. The grounding for the claim of universality is that we feel that others *ought* to agree with us when we make a taste judgment. Upon the proclamation that a thing is beautiful, we require the same liking from others.

   (b) However, aesthetic judgments are *singular*. The judgment can be about only a particular instance of beauty: "This rose is beautiful." My judgment is not universal over all roses.

   (c) Judgments are grounded intersubjectively. Since the way people think and manipulate knowledge is common to all, there is good reason to expect that each subject will judge like every other subject. Sensory pleasures are relative to individuals, but aesthetic satisfactions have a universal, albeit subjective, ground.

   (3) The Subject

   (a) *Taste* is the ability to judge the agreeable in general. The judgment of taste states a relation between the representation (of the object) and a special *disinterested* satisfaction.

   (b) *Disinterest* describes that state in which we have no interests in the real existence of the object. When we contemplate a work of art, we contemplate it without any other concept, and we gain pleasure merely from contemplating it. In order to judge in matters of taste, we must not be in the least biased in favor of the thing's existence but must be wholly indifferent about it. Disinterest is necessary for the universality we expect.

(c)   We appreciate aesthetic objects through a free play of the understanding and the imagination. Free-play judging is judging without bringing the object under any concept. Aesthetic pleasure combines the characteristics of desire (sentiment) and knowledge.

(4)   The Object

(a)   Beauty is an object's form of purposiveness insofar as it is perceived in the object without the presentation of a purpose (purposiveness without purpose). We can observe a purposiveness as to form and take note of it in objects *without* basing it on a purpose. This is beauty.

(b)   Objects must be regarded on their own, and not under any concept. If we judge objects merely in terms of concepts, then we lose all presentation of beauty. This is why there can be no rule or principle by which someone could be compelled to acknowledge that something is beautiful.

(c)   So, for an object to be a beautiful or aesthetically good object is for it to

(i)   be viewed disinterestedly,

(ii)   be viewed with free play between the imagination and the understanding,

(iii) be viewed under no particular category,

(iv)   be viewed as purposive in design, yet with no actual purpose in the real world, and finally,

(v)   be such that if viewed in these ways will produce a favorable judgment, which we expect to be shared by all other properly disposed judges, partly on the basis that everyone has the same "cognitive structures" for aesthetic judging.

(5)   Diversity among Judgments

(a)   Differences among judgments occur because one is exercising a judgment of taste and the other a judgment of "agreeableness" (whether she merely *likes* the object or not) *or* she is judging by "dependent" beauty.

(b)   Kant makes a distinction between free and dependent beauty: free beauty is bracketed off from all instances of that kind; dependent beauty is beauty judged relative to instances of the kind of what ever object is being judged. Free beauty is judging on the basis of the formal features; dependent beauty is judging on the function of the object.

(6)   The "sublime" for Kant is the feeling of the grandeur of reason itself and of man's moral destiny. This arises in two ways:

       (a) when we are confronted in nature with the extremely vast, our imagination falters in the task of comprehending it and we become aware of the supremacy of reason whose ideas reach toward infinite totality, and

       (b) when we are confronted with the overwhelmingly powerful, the weakness of our empirical selves makes us aware of our worth as moral beings.

(7) Problems

       (a) We can empirically investigate whether we would all indeed judge alike if we met all of Kant's viewing-conditions. The difficulty lies in the improbability of Kant being correct. Even if I and my friend are thoroughly disinterested (etc.), we may still, it would seem, differ in our aesthetic judgments.

       (b) Another difficulty is found in examining the Kantian notion of "disinterest." By "disinterested," Kant means that we must attend to the object without any care to its actual existence. But surely we are interested in having continued access to the object, which gives rise to our aesthetic experience of its "contemplative-image." Moreover, this advice seems to put us in the strange position of believing the image or thought-representation of the object to be more valuable than the original.

IV. GERMAN IDEALISM

A. **Friedrich Schiller** (1759–1805)

(1) Schiller was interested in the aesthetic education of mankind. His purpose was to encourage moral education through art. It was a synthesis of art and morality: beauty is the symbol of morality.

(2) Schiller said that through art and beauty we advance from a sensuous to a rational and thereby fully human stage of existence.

B. **Friedrich Schelling** (1775–1854)

(1) Like Kant, he believed that organisms and works of art are alike in that they can be properly understood only *teleologically*, that is, in which the parts serve the whole and the whole is itself purposive.

(2) In art, intelligence for the first time becomes completely self-conscious. Shelling attempted a reconciliation of all oppositions between the self and nature though the idea of art. In the artistic intuition the self is both conscious and unconscious at once.

C. **Georg Wilhelm Friedrich Hegel** (1770–1831)

(1) The Purpose of Art is to make humans understand themselves. Art is born of an attempt by humans to humanize the materials that they find around them. In giving creative form to such materials, they make them less alien. Moreover, art embodies the ideas of the mind in an external form.

(2) Hegel tries to avoid two extremes: that of formulating an abstract philosophy of beauty that would have little relevance to actual art

objects, and that of limiting attention to the purely empirical study of works of art.

(3)   Hegel deals exclusively with artifactual beauty, not natural beauty. "The Absolute Idea of God is more honored by what the mind does or makes than by the productions or formations of nature." Natural beauty is capable of embodying the idea to some degree, but in human art the highest embodiment takes place. Natural beauty is defective because it cannot represent the unity of a spiritual being at every point of the sensuous shape. However concrete the artforms, they are made different for having passed through mind.

(4)   Beauty is the mediation between the sensible and the rational. Beauty is the Idea made sensorily perceptible. [The "Idea" is the result or highest state of dialectical development; "dialectical development" refers to Hegel's (popularized) view that things progress through the process by which the Thesis—one notion—and the Antithesis—a divergence notion—meet to become the Synthesis—a higher notion than the two before. The Synthesis then becomes another Thesis, and the process continues.]

(5)   Categorization of the History of Art

    (a)   Oriental Symbolic Art is where the Idea is overwhelmed by the medium. This is the least valuable art of the three categories.

    (b)   Classical Art is where the Idea and the medium are in harmony. Classical Art is characterized by the divine ideal in sculptures of the human body. These works have independence and completeness.

    (c)   Romantic Art is where the Idea dominates the medium and the spiritualization is complete. This art is the most free, the most spiritual. Romantic art turns away from the external world and thereby achieves the Synthesis between form and content by looking at the inner world.

V.   SOCIALIST REALISM

A.   **Karl Marx** (1818–1883)

(1)   Art belongs to the superstructures of society and is determined by sociohistorical conditions, especially economic condition.

(2)   Beauty is objective, but appreciation is relative to class.

(3)   Art should support the political state by celebrating the values of the proletariat, of the worker, of commonality, good-will, and dedication.

VI.   ROMANTICISM

A.   Introduction

(1)   Romanticism was anti-Enlightenment. While the Enlightenment was action oriented, Romanticism remained contented with sentiment and artistic expression.

(2)   The Romantics conceived of art as essentially the expression of the artist's personal emotions.

(3)   The notion that the work of art was a symbol, a sensuous embodiment of a spiritual meaning, came in to Romanticism.

(4)   From 1820 to 1830, the elevation of the artist led to the notion of *art for art's sake*.

B. **Arthur Schopenhauer** (1788–1860)

(1)   Schopenhauer was a Platonist. He believed that the Platonic realm of Ideas or Forms was true reality; the work was just a mirror of this. It is through art that we are able to consider these Platonic Forms: In art, we are presented with the "permanent essential forms of the world and all its phenomena."

(2)   The "*Will*" is the *will-to-live*; it is desire for the necessities and comforts of survival. Although the Will itself is unknowable, it manifests itself in all want, deficiency, and suffering. It objectifies itself in every action we take, for every action is geared toward our own survival and satisfaction. However, the irony is that we can never be satisfied. In the physical world, the norm is "want" and the more we try to evade want, the less we are able to do so. To struggle is to reinforce the Will as the harbinger of unhappiness and strife in our lives.

(3)   There are only two ways to escape the Will.

    (a)   The first way is through a life of asceticism, with a complete devotion to things spiritual or contemplative and a rejection of all things sensual.

    (b)   The second way is through art. The knowledge of beauty comes through complete alienation from the Will. The artist's concern is with contemplation or Will-less perception. The only consolation life offers to ease the burden of the Will is art. Through art we rise above the particular and contemplate the Forms. But art is temporary relief only.

(4)   This alienation from the Will is characterized by the notion of *disinterest*. Through viewing objects disinterestedly, we view them apart from desire. This allows us to escape willing.

(5)   Schopenhauer ranked the arts. Those with the greatest ability to escape the Will ranked at the top. Architecture was at the bottom, then poetry and tragedy. At the very top stood music, especially formal music such as Baroque. Unlike other arts, music directly expresses the Will itself, not the ideas that are means to the Will.

(6)   Artistic Genius is the capacity of a person to see objects in a different light than his commonplace counterparts. The person of genius requires imagination in order to see in things the Forms. All have some degree of genius in them, in order to appreciate art at all. But most do not have enough to produce art.

   C.　**Friedrich Nietzsche** (1844–1900)

      (1)　There are two energies that burst forth from nature:

         (a)　the Apollonian: Nietzsche calls Apollo the god of all plastic energies. Apollo represents artifactuality, individuation, labor, structure, and symmetry.

         (b)　the Dionysian: Dionysus represents the antithesis of Apollo. Dionysus represents the death of individuation and structure; he represents the freedom of expression, revelry, excitement, spontaneity, and liveliness.

      (2)　It is through the reconciliation of these two energies, the one toward form, the other toward expression, that signals the birth of the best art. This reconciliation happens through the artist and her creative processes. The reconciliation of the two is the most important moment of Greek history.

      (3)　The arts generally make life possible and worth living. Art is integrally bound up with life and living. The art impulses are in nature and are natural in humans. Art is not mere imitation but a sort of metaphysical complement to reality. Art overcomes and transfigures. Nietzsche's definition of art then is active, not passive or static but functionary.

      (4)　Tragedy arises from the conjunction of the two fundamental impulses, the Dionysian and the Apollonian, one a joyful acceptance of experience, the other a need for order and proportion. Tragic art provides us with a way of apprehending this reality that enables us to come to terms with it. Tragic art may thus be said to accomplish the Apollonianization of the Dionysian. Tragedy exists not to inculcate resignation and negation of life, but to affirm life in all its pain to express the artist's "Will to Power."

      (5)　Like Schopenhauer, Nietzsche had a concept of Will, but unlike Schopenhauer, Nietzsche's Will was not a negative, pessimistic force. Nietzsche's Will is full of life, creativity, and power.

   D.　Problems with Romanticism

      (1)　If art is essentially the vital expression of emotion, is it that *all* vital expression of emotion is art? What about "soap-box rantings" (a vital expression of emotion)?

      (2)　And if art is essentially the vital expression of emotion, does this mean that *all* art must be a vital expression of emotion? What do we do with formalistic art?

VII.　EXPRESSIONISM

   A.　Introduction

      (1)　The 18th- and 19th-century Romantics made the expression of emotion all important. Wordsworth said that all good poetry is the spontaneous overflow of powerful feelings.

      (2)　The Expressionists attempt to determine the *nature* of the expression of the artist. Simply saying that it is an overflow of emotion is insufficient.

B. **Leo Tolstoy** (1855–1936)

    (1)   Art is essentially a form of communication—the transmission of emotion—and the emotion must be universal.

    (2)   It is first necessary, in defining art, to cease to consider it as a means to pleasure and to consider it as one of the conditions of human life. Every work of art causes the receiver to enter into a certain kind of relationship both with the artist and with all who before during or after receive the same artistic impression. It is upon this capacity of persons to receive another person's expression of feeling and experience those feelings himself, that the activity of art is based.

    (3)   To evoke in oneself a feeling one has once experienced, and having evoked it in oneself, then, by means of movements, lines, colors, sounds, or forms expressed in words, so to transmit that feeling that other may experience this same feeling—this is the activity of art. Art is a human activity consisting in this, that one person consciously, by means of certain external signs, passes on to others feeling he has lived through, and that other people are infect by these feelings and also experience them.

    (4)   "The degree of infectiousness is the sole measure of excellence in art." The emotion sought to be communicated must be individualized, must be very clear, and must be as sincere as the artist herself felt it (sincerity is most important).

    (5)   The meaning of life, the religious perception of a society, is expressed by the best artists.

    (6)   For an object to be a work of art is for it to

        (a)   be an "infectious" form of communication of sincerely felt universal emotion,

        (b)   invoke sincere feeling in its audience, and

        (c)   accord with the religious environment in which it is created.

    (7)   Problems

        (a)   It is a common ingredient in much art, especially lately, that instead of supporting the religious climate, it *challenges* this climate.

        (b)   A second problem for Tolstoy is the infectious of *actual* feeling. Although the condition to communicate emotion is standard to the tradition of Expressionism, the edict to *infect* the audience with a *sincere* level of the feeling being expressed leaves us expecting perhaps too much from the artist or her work.

C. **Benedetto Croce** (1866–1952)

    (1)   The aesthetic experience is a primitive form of *cognitive* experience. Croce was opposed to Romanticism. He did not identify intuitions as feelings; "Feeling" was too ambiguous.

    (2)   Aesthetics is the science of images or intuitive knowledge. At the lower limit of consciousness are raw sense impressions, which when clarified are *intuitions*. An intuition is not an instinctive

knowing or a grasp of self-evident truth. It is rather an inner vision of an image, an immediate knowledge through the imagination of an individual concrete thing.

(3)   To express these intuitions is to create art. Unsuccessful expression is not that a fully formed intuition has not been fully expressed, but that an impression has not been fully intuited.

(4)   The work of art does not exist objectively in an external world. The work of art exists in the expression of the artist, in her intention. Intuition and expression are identical. Expression is *not* the same as communication or the embodiment of the external physical thing. The work of art is not a physical thing, but a mental re-creation. The physical work is merely the vehicle of transmitting the expression.

(5)   Pure imitation is not art, though it may be respectable. The artist does not feel and create without thinking, willing, and acting. The basis of all art is human personality.

D. **R.G. Collingwood** (1889–1943)

(1)   Collingwood determines that (i) art has something to do with making things, and (ii) art has something to do with arousing emotion, though is not, he hastens to add, synonymous with it.

(2)   It is, he agrees with Croce, naive to say that an artist merely expresses emotion. This idea seems to presuppose that the artist has some emotion that she cannot identify, and through the expression that would be the creation of an art work, she either discovers it or purges herself of it.

(3)   He sees the expression of emotion having definite elements, some of the necessary ones being

    (a)   that the emotion is not simply mentioned to the audience, but is *demonstrated* to them,

    (b)   the emotion is individualized, is this emotion *here and now*, not just one of a species, say, of happiness or sadness, and

    (c)   the expression is not simply for the arousal of emotion, the expression of emotion which is art is not *manipulative*. The artist must be absolutely candid with his audience. He must not rant, rave, or preach, but gently and subtly communicate the specific, unique emotion that he wishes to express.

(4)   Perfect beauty lies between the two poles of sublimity and comedy. Real beauty is neither wholly objective nor subjective in any sense that excludes the work. It is an experience in which the mind and the object are intimately related.

E. Problems with Expressionism

(1)   In Expressionism the audience is supposed to re-create the intention of the artist, but is it really possible to re-create what the artist felt/thought? How can we know if we have "got it right"?

(2) What about those cases where the artist really *does not know* what she is attempting to express? What if her expression is of something from her subconscious? What if it is a matter of acculturation of which she is not consciously aware?

VIII. AMERICAN NATURALISM

A. Introduction

(1) By "Naturalism" we do not mean something like a theory of beauty where what is most beautiful is what is most natural. Perhaps the simplest explanation of the notion is that naturalism is committed to explaining the world from a materialist or scientific perspective.

(2) In discussing aesthetics, the Naturalist pays a good deal more attention to the empirical inquiries conducted by psychology (and other sciences).

B. **George Santayana** (1863–1952)

(1) Santayana's method is psychological, not historical or didactic. Aesthetics is concerned with the perception of values that depend upon emotional consciousness (appreciations, appetite, and preferences).

(2) Pleasure is the essence of the perception of beauty. The pleasure of aesthetics cannot be divorced from interests.

(3) At each point, beauty rests on human feelings and human interests. Beauty is a subjective phenomenon, *the objectification of pleasure*. The beauty we attribute to objects is not in the objects, it is in us. Beauty is pleasure objectified.

(4) Beauty of form arises from a conscious synthesis of distinguishable parts in a unified whole.

(5) These is great disagreement among judgments, and similarities can be accounted for by similar upbringing and similar societies. It is meaningless to say that what is beautiful to one person *ought* to be beautiful to another. The claim to universality rests on the mistake that beauty is an objective property.

(6) Problems

   (a) This theory is highly subjectivistic. It makes no provision for deciding which of two conflicting judgments is right (supposing that they are not both wrong).

   (b) Another problem is that there seem to be a great host of items that seem quite pleasurable, but that do not seem particularly aesthetic.

C. **John Dewey** (1859–1952)

(1) Dewey focuses not on aesthetic objects, but on the aesthetic experience.

(2) Dewey uses the term 'experience' in two ways:

   (a) The first is to indicate the interactive relationship between the individual and the world around her.

    (b)   The second way is to indicate a special sort of the first kind. This special sort Dewey calls *an* experience. *An* experience is any experience that principally has the characteristic of being unified and complete.

(3)   Any experience—regardless of whether it is *an* experience or just a garden-variety experience—is aesthetic to some degree, specifically, to the degree that it incorporates *unity*. But not every experience is as aesthetic as every other experience, because the degree of unity will vary from experience to experience.

(4)   Those experiences that are truly aesthetic in character are those experiences that fit into his classification of *an* experience. It is those experiences that are *maximally* unified that are truly aesthetic experiences. When a moment is sufficient to itself, is individualized, this is *an* experience.

(5)   The judgment of whether an experience is *an* experience is not found in some metaphysical system. The judgment is made solely on the basis of the felt experience of the individual perceiver.

(6)   The most enduring aesthetic objects are those that provide the richest aesthetic experience or create most frequently *an* experience.

(7)   When the common experience of humans is taken as basic, the focus is not on her divorce from interest in the objects she believes are aesthetic. Quite the reverse: Dewey shows a common man who is vitally interested in the objects that he experiences aesthetically, and the interest and attention that he invests the objects with are just those characteristics that lead him to experience the object aesthetically.

(8)   Aesthetics is a much broader field for Dewey than it is for most other aestheticians. For him, hard lines between aesthetic and non-aesthetic experience, as traditionally viewed, are blurred.

IX.   FORMALISTS

A.   Introduction

(1)   Formalism as a theory of criticism is a recent view, made famous by the school known as the New Critics. Unlike its predecessors, Formalism takes seriously the problem of "artist intention." The Formalist seeks to treat the aesthetic object as divorced from its origins and other relations she believes irrelevant.

(2)   We are here interested in the objective properties, particularly the internal formal relations, of aesthetic objects.

B.   George Edward Moore (1873–1958)

(1)   Aesthetic enjoyments and personal affections include all the greatest and by far the greatest goods we can imagine.

(2)   Objective beauty is found in objects possessing *organic unity* or wholeness. Parts of artworks themselves may have a certain value,

but when they are put all together, the value of the whole is greater than the sum of the parts.

(3)   The success of the unity is the criterion of evaluation of the work as art.

C.   **Clive Bell** (1881–1964)

(1)   The starting point for any system of aesthetics must be the personal experience of a peculiar (aesthetic) emotion—the provokers of this emotion are works of art. The common quality that is peculiar to all objects that provoke it is the central problem of aesthetics.

(2)   The relations and combinations of lines and colors, certain forms and relations of forms, stir our aesthetic emotions. These aesthetically moving forms he calls *Significant Form.*

(3)   The presence of Significant Form elicits in us aesthetic emotion. Before we feel aesthetic emotion, we perceive the rightness and necessity of the combination. Significant Form is present only when the aesthetic emotion is experienced.

(4)   Significant Form is not beauty. Beauty is a broader category; natural objects can be beautiful. Significant Form elicits an emotion that is different from the emotion we get when we look at something beautiful.

(5)   The most moving form of art is what scholars call "primitive." Primitives neither create illusions nor make display of extravagant accomplishment, but concentrate their energies on the one thing needful—the creation of form.

(6)   Problems

(a)   The theory seems very subjective: If I "see" Significant Form in an object and you do not, then the object might be art for me, but not for you.

(b)   The account may be circular: The presence of Significant Form is only detected when one experiences the "Significant Form Emotion." But the only way to experience the "Significant Form Emotion" is to be in attendance to some work with Significant Form. The Significant Form, then, does little work to define the Significant-Form-Emotion, since the Significant-Form-Emotion is defined in terms of the Significant Form.

D.   **Monroe Beardsley** (1915–1985)

(1)   Beardsley was a Formalist, but principally with regard to aesthetic interpretation and aesthetic judgment, not with the establishment of some object as a work of art. In discussing aesthetic experiences and aesthetic value, Beardsley might better be labeled a Naturalist.

(2)   The *Intentional Fallacy* states that we do not need to know, nor can we on most occasions, what was in the mind of the artist in order to

interpret the artwork. The correct interpretation is the one which is determined by rules of language.

(3)   Beardsley's focus is not the aesthetic object per se, but the *aesthetic experience*, or the relationship between the perceiver and the object. The aesthetic experience is characterized in that the viewer's attention is focused on the formal qualities of the object, and her psychological state is characterized by unity and pleasure.

(4)   The object is evaluated against the following criteria: For an object to be an aesthetically good object is for it to

   (a)   be unified,

   (b)   and/or intense,

   (c)   and/or complex, and

   (d)   be such that it prompts in attentive perceivers a pleasurable experience characterized by unity, and/or intensity, and/or complexity.

(5)   One problem is that it is not clear that aesthetic experiences—not to mentioned criticism and interpretation—cannot be enriched through an appreciation of certain facts about the origins of works of art, or the relations of that work to others.

E.   Problems with Formalism

(1)   First, although it is easy to concentrate on the form of something like a musical composition, it is difficult to view a visual work that is obviously a representation purely as a formal construct.

(2)   It is not clear what the value of simply looking at the formal properties of artworks is. Why not pay attention to the fact that the work actually does represent X ?

X.   ANTIESSENTIALISM

A.   Introduction

(1)   Chronologically, the trend toward Antiessentialism began much earlier than the latter 20th century.

(2)   The Antiessentialists contend that there is no definition that can be given for what all works of art share, or what their common nature is, but that a counterexample cannot be found. There are two central lines of argument:

   (a)   Either there is simply no hope of developing an "essential" definition of art, that art is an "open concept" or something along those lines, or

   (b)   there are *many* definitions that equally well apply to art, some definitions to some kinds of art, other definitions to other kinds of art, with a sort of series of threads running throughout.

B.   **Ludwig Wittgenstein** (1889–1951)

(1)   It must first be understood that Wittgenstein did not, regarding Antiessentialism, explicitly discuss *art*. However, his influence was great and deserves attention here.

(2)   Wittgenstein would not contend that patterns, resemblances, general common features, and so forth cannot be found among differing objects all (apparently) correctly labeled 'art'. The problem is that when any single one of these patterns or common features is explored as a possible definition of art, counterexamples are always forthcoming.

(3)   Wittgenstein introduces his theory of "family resemblances." A family resemblance may be explained in a couple of ways.

   (a)   First, consider your own family. While your brothers and sisters all bear some resemblance to yourself and to your parents, they do not all resemble each other in every detail. Furthermore, it may be the case that while your brother has features that each of your parents have, and you do too, you have *no* features in common with your brother. But you are still related to him.

   (b)   Consider "games." Try as we will, it is nearly impossible to give any definition of 'game' that will not find some counterexample. Some are based on chance, some on skill. However, it is not hard to adequately and noncontroversially identify objects as 'games'. We can apply the label well, though we cannot articulate the commonality.

(4)   Perhaps artworks, while all equally correctly labeled 'art', share no single feature, but share a group of features, each instance of art having some of the features common to other artworks but missing some features that other artworks have.

(5)   This sort of definition is a "disjunctive definition," because it is composed of "disjuncts": separate definitions separated by the connective 'or'. Any one of these disjuncts, when applicable, is all that an object need possess in order to rightly be called 'art'. If none of the disjuncts applies, then the object is not art. If one or more applies, then the object *is* art.

C. **Morris Weitz**

(1)   This sort of "disjunctive definition" project is also pursued by Morris Weitz, an aesthetician working today.

(2)   He suggests this not primarily because of the wealth of counterexamples that can seemingly be leveled at any given definition, but because 'art' itself is a concept that continues to grow and change. It continues to "evolve." Art is an *open concept*. Instead of saying that all artworks will fit into the categories/definitions mentioned in some (finite) set of disjuncts, Weitz contends that this set of disjuncts itself must be "open," that it must admit of new disjuncts, so that not only instances of art can evolve, but the categories in which they fall can also grow and change.

XI. SYMBOLISM

   A. Introduction

      (1)   Theories of Symbolism are recent, having come on the scene in the latter half of the 20th century.

(2) Each of these two views treats art as a symbol or sign. The question is, As a symbol of what?

B. **Nelson Goodman** (b. 1906)

(1) For Goodman, art functions as a symbol. Artworks incorporate symbols which we recognize as denoting items in the world. Artworks employ symbols which conventionally denote items in the world. They are recognized to denote the items they do denote not because of a resemblance relationship, but because of a matter of convention. Essentially, Goodman's theory might also be called a *representational* theory.

(2) Speakers of the "language of art," then, understand what the symbols denote, and they accomplish this understanding by understanding the conventions in which art functions. For us to understand art, to *see it as art*, is for us to be speakers of this art-language, to recognize that certain symbols denote certain items.

(3) It is important to understand that while Goodman's theory has a relationship to theories of Representation, his is properly not an *Imitation/Mimesis* theory. This is so because Goodman does not see *imitation* as artistic. It incorporates no symbols, but simply depicts, in as exact a manner as possible (or as exact as the artist can manage) what is really there in the world.

C. **Suzanne Langer** (1895–1985)

(1) Langer's analysis, while still a view in the Symbolism tradition, is markedly different from Goodman's. Langer's view incorporates views from both Expressionism and Formalism.

(2) For an object to be an art object is for it to be a symbol of a formal treatment of some emotion that the artist sought to express.

(3) For Langer, artworks are symbols of human feeling. However, they are not of emotions themselves, but of the "formal features" of these emotions. Artworks symbolize emotion in an articulate, organized way. Art symbols *express*.

(4) Formalism is incorporated into the analysis through Langer's belief that the emotion which is expressed—in a coherent, developed way—is expressed through the *form* of the work. Through the form of the work, the artist conveys the emotion that she wishes.

XII. INSTITUTIONALISTS / ARTWORLD THEORISTS

A. Introduction

(1) Antiessentialism may be seen as the motivation behind the theory of art that I will call the Artworld Theory. The Artworld theorists argue that Antiessentialism is incorrect, that art is *not* *in*definable.

(2) They argue that while there may not be a nature common to all artworks per se, that is, as objects, there is something which is common to all artworks: their position in the Artworld or the Art Institution.

B. **Arthur Danto** (b. 1924)

    (1) We must first have a means for *recognizing* art. Danto notes the work of such artists as Marcel Duchamp, Robert Rauschenberg, and Andy Warhol. What accounts for the difference between the Warhol Brillo pad box and the one in the supermarket is a *theory of art*. Without a theory of art, the Warhol box and the supermarket box would not be different. The Warhol box is *interpreted* as a work of art. The supermarket box is not. And it is the application of the interpretation *as art* that makes for the difference.

    (2) The interpretation can transform, or as Danto puts it, can transfigure the commonplace into art. Without interpretation, there is no art.

    (3) For there to exist a "transfigurative" or "artful" interpretation is for that interpretation to be *made through* the Artworld, and to be *accepted* by the Artworld. The Artworld is a living, changing *historically based tradition*, a "subjective collective," consisting of artists, critics, patrons, audiences, art historians, curators, producers/ directors, "art guild" members, aestheticians, and probably sociologists and anthropologists, *and* consisting of them *over time*. The Artworld may be described as a *tradition*, an institution not merely made up of people and objects, but of these things through time, of the interpretive tradition itself.

C. **George Dickie** (b. 1926)

    (1) The institutional structure in which the art object is embedded, not the different kinds of appreciation, makes the difference between the appreciation of art and the appreciation of non-art. When Dickie calls the artworld an institution, he is saying that it is an established practice, not that it is an established society or corporation. We cannot know all about the artworld. The artworld might be the presenters and the goers. This is simpler than Danto's conception; Dickie's Art Institution is of the here and now.

    (2) Artworks are artifacts to be presented to the artworld. A work of art in the classificatory sense is

        (a) an artifact and

        (b) a "candidate for appreciation by some person or person acting on behalf of a certain social institution" (the Artworld).

    (3) Problems

        (a) If a thing is art if it is appreciated, then does this disallow anything from being bad art? No, Dickie means only that a thing is meant to be appreciated or has some potential of being appreciated.

        (b) Some claim that Dickie's definition of artist and artworld are circular. It would seem that the Artworld is defined in terms of its membership (such as artists, audiences, and critics). However, artists and others are defined in terms of their relations with certain objects: artworks. And then artworks are defined only in terms of their acceptance by the Artworld. It would seem that there is not a clear foundation, some one category or subset of the set 'Artworld' that can be defined without recourse back to some other part of the Artworld.

XIII. DECONSTRUCTIONISM

A. Deconstructionists like **Jacques Derrida, Paul DeMan,** and **Stanley Fish** suggest that the question *What does this work mean?* is misadvised. First, we cannot come to understand *the* meaning of the object, since there is no single meaning to be found. If we mean what was in the artist's mind, then we are struck with the difficulty of accessing the intentions of artists perhaps long dead. And if we are interested in living artists, we still must contend with the very real possibilities that

(1) there are elements that *mean* something in the work that are/were not in the artist's conscious mind; perhaps she is expressing something with hidden, say, Freudian meanings; perhaps she constructs something that means more than what she could have, either consciously or unconsciously, put into it.

(2) Perhaps there are elements in the work that the artist did not consciously intend to put there, but that the society or context in which she lives and works has in some sense *conditioned* her to accept and express. Perhaps there are value-laden overtones, of which the artist is not conscious but that are nonetheless detectable by interpreters (or critics).

B. Furthermore, the question *What is the meaning?* is misadvised because there are indeed *many* meanings. And in the presentation of different meanings the conventions of symbolism and the expectations of those doing the interpreting are revealed. With different interpreters—with different backgrounds—different interpretations can be found, and given the diversity in grounding each one, a decision about which of two is the best is not only impossible, but also ludicrous. We do not take the artist, determine her intent, and have the meaning. This is to overlook a great deal. Nor can we take the object, and in attending to it closely, understand its meaning. Meaning is not objective; meaning is subjective. And with the subjectivity comes a huge wealth of possibilities in terms of interpretation, and all perhaps relative to a single object.

Bibliography

Adams, Elizabeth. *The Aesthetic Experience.* Chicago: University of Chicago Press, 1907.

Aldrich, Virgil C. "Aesthetic Perception and Objectivity." *British Journal of Aesthetics* 18, (1978): 209–216.

Aldrich, Virgil C. "Back to Aesthetic Experience." *Journal of Aesthetics and Art Criticism* 24, (1966): 365–372.

Aldrich, Virgil C. *Philosophy of Art.* Englewood Cliffs, NJ: Prentice Hall, 1963.

Alexander, Thomas. *John Dewey's Theory of Art, Experience, and Nature.* Albany: State University of New York, 1987.

Aristotle. *The Poetics.* Indianapolis: Hackett, 1987. Richard Janko, translator.

Battin, Margaret, John Fisher, Ronald Moore, and Anita Silvers. *Puzzles about Art: An Aesthetics Casebook.* New York: St. Martin's Press, 1989.

Beardsley, Monroe C. "Aesthetic Experience Regained." *Journal of Aesthetics and Art Criticism* 28, (1969): 3–11.

Beardsley, Monroe C. *The Aesthetic Point of View.* Ithaca: Cornell University, 1982.

Beardsley, Monroe C. *Aesthetics: Problems in the Philosophy of Criticism.* Indianapolis: Hackett, 1981.

Beardsley, Monroe C. "On the Creation of Art." *Journal of Aesthetics and Art Criticism* 23, (1965): 291–304.

Beardsley, Monroe C. "What Is an Aesthetic Quality?" *Theoria* 39, (1973): 50–70.

Beardsley, Monroe C. and William Wimsatt. "The Intentional Fallacy." *Sewanee Review* 54, (1946): 3–23.

Bell, Clive. *Art.* London: Chatto and Windus, 1914.

Blocker, H. G. "A New Look at Aesthetic Distance." *British Journal of Aesthetics* 17, (1977): 219–229.

Bullough, Edward. "'Psychical Distance' as a Factor in Art and as an Aesthetic Principle." *British Journal of Psychology* 5, (1912): 87–117.

Bullough, Edward. *Aesthetics: Lectures and Essays.* Stanford, CA: Stanford University Press, 1957.

Burke, Edmund. *Philosophical Enquiry into the Origin of our Ideas of the Sublime and Beautiful.* Oxford: Oxford University Press, 1998 (1757).

Carroll, Noel. "Clive Bell's Aesthetic Hypothesis." George Dickie, Richard Sclafani, and Robert Roblin, eds. *Aesthetics: A Critical Anthology.* 2nd ed. New York: St. Martin's Press, 1989.

Cohen, Marshall. "Appearance and the Aesthetic Attitude." *Journal of Philosophy* 56, (1959): 915–925.

Cohen, Ted. "The Possibility of Art." *Philosophical Review* 38, (1973): 69–82.

Collingwood, R.G. *The Principles of Art.* Oxford: Clarendon Press, 1938.

Croce, Benedetto. *Aesthetic.* London: Heinemann, 1921.

Danto, Arthur. "The Artworld." *Journal of Philosophy* 61, (1964): 571–584.

Danto, Arthur. "Deep Interpretation." *Journal of Philosophy* 78, (1981): 691–705.

Danto, Arthur. *The Philosophical Disenfranchisement of Art.* New York: Columbia University Press, 1986.

Danto, Arthur. *The Transfiguration of the Commonplace.* Cambridge, MA: Harvard University Press, 1981.

Dawson, Sheila. "'Distancing' as an Aesthetic Principle." *Australasian Journal of Philosophy* 39, (1961): 155–174.

Dewey, John. *Art as Experience.* New York: Perigee, 1934.

Dewey, John. *Experience and Nature.* New York: Dover, 1958.

Dickie, George. *Art and the Aesthetic: An Institutional Analysis.* Ithaca: Cornell University Press, 1974.

Dickie, George. "Attitude and Object: Aldrich on the Aesthetic." *Journal of Aesthetics and Art Criticism* 25, (1966): 89–92.

Dickie, George. "Beardsley's Phantom Aesthetic Experience." *Journal of Philosophy* 62, (1965): 129–135.

Dickie, George. "Beardsley's Theory of Aesthetic Experience." *Journal of Aesthetic Education* 8, (1974): 13–23.

Dickie, George. "Bullough and the Concept of Psychical Distance." *Philosophy and Phenomenological Research* 22, (1961): 233–238.

Dickie, George. *Evaluating Art.* Philadelphia: Temple University, 1988.

Dickie, George. "The Myth of the Aesthetic Attitude." *American Philosophical Quarterly* 1, (1964): 56–65.

Dickie, George. "Stolnitzs' Attitude: Taste and Perception." *Journal of Aesthetics and Art Criticism* 43, (1984): 195–204.

Diffey, T.J. *Tolstoy's What Is Art?* London: Croom Helm, 1985.

Ducasse, Curt. *The Philosophy of Art.* New York: Dover, 1929.

Dutton, Dennis. *The Forger's Art.* Berkeley: University of California Press, 1983.

Eaton, Marcia. "Good and Correct Interpretations." *Journal of Aesthetics and Art Criticism* 29, (1970): 227–234.

Fenner, David. *The Aesthetic Attitude.* Atlantic Highlands, NJ: Humanities Press, 1996.

Fisher, John. "Did Plato Have a Theory of Art?" *Pacific Philosophical Quarterly* 63, (1982): 93–99.

Fry, Roger. *Vision and Design.* New York: Brentano's, 1924.

Gaut, Berys. "Interpreting the Arts: A Patchwork Theory." *Journal of Aesthetics and Art Criticism* 51(4), (1993): 597–609.

Glickman, Jack. "Creativity in the Arts." Joseph Margolis, ed. *Philosophy Looks at the Arts*. 2nd ed. Philadelphia: Temple University Press, 1978.

Goldman, Alan. *Aesthetic Value*. Boulder, CO: Westview Press, 1995.

Goldman, Alan. "On Interpreting Art and Literature." *Journal of Aesthetics and Art Criticism* 48, (1990): 205–214.

Goldman, Alan. "Properties, Aesthetic," David Cooper, ed. *A Companion to Aesthetics*. Oxford: Blackwell Publishers, 1992.

Gombrich, E. H. *Art and Illusion*. New York: Pantheon, 1960.

Goodman, Nelson. *Languages of Art*. Indianapolis: Hackett, 1976.

Hospers, John. "Implied Truths in Literature." *Journal of Aesthetics and Art Criticism* 19, (1960): 37–46.

Hospers, John. *Meaning and Truth in the Arts*. Chapel Hill: University of North Carolina Press, 1946.

Hume, David. *An Inquiry into the Principles of Morals*. New York: E. P. Dutton, 1956.

Hume, David. "Of the Standard of Taste." *Four Dissertations*. New York: Garland, 1970 (1757).

Hutcheson, Francis. *An Inquiry into the Original of Our Ideas of Beauty and Virtue*. New York: Garland, 1971.

Isenberg, Arnold. "Critical Communication." *Philosophical Review* 58, (July 1949): 330–344.

Kamins, Herbert. "Reply to Prof. Weitz." *Philosophical Review* 61, (1952): 66–71.

Kant, Immanuel. *Critique of Judgment*. Indianapolis: Hackett, 1987.

Kivy, Peter. "Aesthetic Aspects and Aesthetic Qualities." *Journal of Philosophy* 65, (1968): 85–93.

Kivy, Peter. *Francis Hutcheson: An Inquiry Concerning Beauty, Order, Harmony and Design*. Hague: Martinus Nijhoff, 1973.

Langer, Suzanne. *Feeling and Form*. London: Scribners, 1953.

Langer, Susanne. *Philosophy in a New Key*. Cambridge, MA: Harvard University, 1951.

Loftin, Robert. "Psychical Distance and the Aesthetic Appreciation of Wilderness." *International Journal of Applied Philosophy* 3, (1986): 15–19.

Mandelbaum, Maurice. "Family Resemblances and Generalization Concerning the Arts." *American Philosophical Quarterly* 2, (1965): 219–228.

Margolis, Joseph. "Aesthetic Perception." *Journal of Aesthetics and Art Criticism* 19, (1960): 209–214.

Margolis, Joseph. "Describing and Interpreting Works of Art." *Philosophy and Phenomenological Research* 21, (1961): 537–542.

McCloskey, Mary. *Kant's Aesthetic*. Albany: State University of New York Press, 1987.

Mitias, Michael. "What Makes an Experience Aesthetic?" *Journal of Aesthetics and Art Criticism* 41, (1982): 157–169.

Moore, G. E. *Principia Ethica*. Cambridge, UK: Cambridge University Press, 1903.

Morgan, Douglas. "Creativity Today." *Journal of Aesthetics and Art Criticism* 12, (1953): 1–23.

Morgan, Douglas. "Must Art Tell the Truth?" *Journal of Aesthetics and Art Criticism* 26, (1967): 17–27.

Mothersill, Mary. "Critical Reasons." *Philosophical Quarterly* 2, (1961): 477–485.

Nietzsche, Friedrich. *Birth of Tragedy and the Case of Wagner.* Walter Kaufman, trans. New York: Random House, 1967.

Osborne. Harold. "The Elucidation of Aesthetic Experience." *Journal of Aesthetics and Art Criticism* 23, (1964): 145–152.

Papanoutsos, E. "The Aristotelian Katharsis." *British Journal of Aesthetics* 17, (1977): 361–364.

Plato. *Ion* in *Two Comic Dialogues.* Indianapolis: Hackett, 1983.

Plato. *The Republic* (particularly Books II, III, and X). Oxford: Oxford University Press, 1941.

Plato. *The Symposium* included in *The Collected Dialogues of Plato.* Edith Hamilton and Huntington Cairns, eds. Princeton, NJ: Princeton University Press, 1961.

Price, Kingsley. "Is There Artistic Truth?" *Journal of Philosophy* 46, (1949): 285–290.

Puffer, Ethel (Howes). *The Psychology of Beauty.* New York: Houghton Mifflin, 1905.

Santayana, George. *The Sense of Beauty.* New York: Collier Publishing, 1961.

Schlesinger, George. "Aesthetic Experience and the Definition of Art." *British Journal of Aesthetics* 19, (1979): 167–176.

Schopenhauer, Arthur. *The World as Will and Idea.* London: Routledge & Kegan Paul, 1896.

Shaftesbury, Anthony. *Characteristics of Men, Manners, Opinions, Times.* New York: Bobbs-Merrill, 1964.

Sheppard, Anne. *Aesthetics: An Introduction to the Philosophy of Art.* Oxford, UK: Oxford University Press, 1987.

Sibley, Frank. "Aesthetic and Non-aesthetic." *Philosophical Review* 74, (1965): 135–159.

Sibley, Frank. "Aesthetic Concepts." *Philosophical Review* 68, (1959): 421–450.

Stecker, Robert. "The End of an Institutional Definition of Art." *British Journal of Aesthetics* 26, (1986): 124–132.

Stevenson, Charles. "Interpretation and Evaluation in Aesthetics." Max Black, ed. *Philosophical Analysis.* Ithaca: Cornell University Press, 1950.

Stolnitz, Jerome. *Aesthetics and Philosophy of Art Criticism.* New York: Houghton Mifflin, 1960.

Stolnitz, Jerome. "'The Aesthetic Attitude' in the Rise of Modern Aesthetics." *Journal of Aesthetics and Art Criticism* 36, (1978): 409–422.

Stolnitz, Jerome. "On the Origins of 'Aesthetic Disinterestedness'." *Journal of Aesthetics and Art Criticism* 20, (1961): 131–144.

Stolnitz, Jerome. "On the Significance of Lord Shaftesbury in Modern Aesthetic Theory." *Philosophical Quarterly* 11, (1961): 97–113.

Stolnitz, Jerome. "Some Questions Concerning Aesthetic Perception." *Philosophy and Phenomenological Research* 22, (1961): 69–87.

Tollefsen, O. "The Family Resmblances Argument and Definitions of Art." *Journal of Metaphysics* 7, (1976): 206–216.

Tolstoy, Leo. *What Is Art?* Indianapolis: Hackett, 1960.

Tomas, Vincent. "Creativity in Art." *Philosophical Review,* 1952.

Tomas, Vincent, ed. *Creativity in the Arts.* Englewood Cliffs, NJ: Prentice Hall, 1964.

Townsend, Dabney. "From Shaftesbury to Kant: The Development of the Concept of Aesthetic Experience." *Journal of the History of Ideas* 48, (1987): 287–305.

Townsend, Dabney. "Shaftesbury's Aesthetic Theory." *Journal of Aesthetics and Art Criticism* 41, (1982): 205–213.

Tsugawa, Albert. *The Idea of Criticism.* Philadelphia: Pennsylvania State University Press, 1967.

Urmson, J.O. "What Makes a Situation Aesthetic?" Joseph Margolis, ed. *Philosophy Looks at the Arts.* New York: Scribner's, 1962.

Walsh, Dorothy. "The Cognitive Content of Art." *The Philosophical Review* 52, (1943): 433–451.

Walton, Kendall. "Categories of Art." *Philosophical Review* 79, (1970): 334–367.

Weitz, Morris. "Criticism without Evaluation." *Philosophical Review* 61, (1952): 59–65.

Weitz, Morris. *The Opening Mind.* Chicago: University of Chicago Press, 1977.

Weitz, Morris. "Reasons in Criticism." *Journal of Aesthetics and Art Criticism* 20, (1962): 429–437.

Weitz, Morris. "The Role of Theory in Aesthetics." *Journal of Aesthetics and Art Criticism* 15, (1956): 27–35.

Weitz, Morris. "Truth in Literature." *Revue Internationale de Philosophie* 9, (1955): 116–129.

Wittgenstein, Ludwig. *Philosophical Investigations.* New York: MacMillan, 1973.

Ziff, Paul. *Antiaesthetics.* Dordrecht: Reidel, 1984.

Index

About the Author

DAVID E.W. FENNER teaches philosophy at the University of North Florida. He is the author of *The Aesthetic Attitude* and the editor of *Ethics and the Arts* and *Ethics in Education*.